Jun. 2015

From

STUFFED
to
SORTED

Mary Anne Bennie

YOUR ESSENTIAL GUIDE
TO ORGANISING, ROOM BY ROOM

W

John Wiley

First published in 2012 by John Wiley & Sons Australia, Ltd
42 McDougall St, Milton Qld 4064

Office also in Melbourne

Typeset in Quicksand 10.5/13.5

© MaryAnne Bennie 2012

The moral rights of the author have been asserted

National Library of Australia Cataloguing-in-Publication data:

Author:	Bennie, MaryAnne
Title:	From stuffed to sorted: your essential guide to organising, room by room / MaryAnne Bennie
ISBN:	9780730378273 (pbk.)
Notes:	Includes index
Subjects:	House cleaning. Home economics.
Dewey Number:	648.5

Cover design by Suzanne Sunwoo

Cover image: ©PunchStock/MIXA

Paper Flow® is the registered trademark of MaryAnne Bennie

in8® is the registered trademark of in8 Pty Ltd

Printed in China by Printplus Limited

10 9 8 7 6 5 4 3 2 1

Disclaimer
The material in this publication is of the nature of general comment only, and does not represent professional advice. It is not intended to provide specific guidance for particular circumstances and it should not be relied on as the basis for any decision to take action or not take action on any matter which it covers. Readers should obtain professional advice where appropriate, before making any such decision. To the maximum extent permitted by law, the author and publisher disclaim all responsibility and liability to any person, arising directly or indirectly from any person taking or not taking action based on the information in this publication.

Contents

About the author v

A word from the author vi

Introduction vii

PART I Masterclasses

1 **Masterclass 1:** setting up for success 3

2 **Masterclass 2:** the **in8steps** system 9

3 **Masterclass 3:** a space mission 31

4 **Masterclass 4:** getting a handle on hardware 37

5 **Masterclass 5:** time-saving techniques 53

PART II Room by room

6 Bathroom blitz 61

7 Laundry hung and dried 79

8 Kickstart your kitchen 99

9 Bedroom boost 127

10 Fresh faces for living spaces 149

11 Office overhaul 171

12 Lifting the door on garages 187

Acknowledgements 201

About in8 home office and life organising 203

About the author

MaryAnne Bennie is Australia's organising guru. She began her professional organising career after realising that being organised was one of the most valuable, transferrable life skills a person could possess.

MaryAnne is passionate about liberating people from the tyranny of clutter. In 2002 she founded a company called 'in8 home office and life organising' and has since developed systems to keep homes, offices and lives running smoothly.

Her Paper Flow system has already been documented in the best-selling book *Paper Flow: your ultimate guide to making paperwork easy*, co-authored with Brigitte Hinneberg (Wrightbooks 2011). This book shows readers how to manage household, personal and business paperwork. The Paper Flow system is fast becoming the paper management system of choice for people all over the world.

In *From Stuffed to Sorted*, MaryAnne introduces readers to the **in8steps** system and shows how easy it is to apply these steps to totally reorganise the stuff in your life and turn houses back into homes. As a wife, mother and businesswoman, MaryAnne fully understands the struggle to juggle home, office and life. The **in8steps** system is tried and tested and, if followed, will work for everyone regardless of how much stuff or space they have.

Prior to becoming a professional organiser, MaryAnne was a senior lecturer at a leading Australian university. She holds a Bachelor of Education and Master of Business.

MaryAnne's organising expertise is regularly featured in newspapers and magazines, and on websites and radio. She motivates and inspires people, and fully equips them with the information and tools they need to organise their homes, their offices and their lives.

A word from the author

Organising your home is going to change your life forever. Some time ago a client—let's call her Jane—called me in and asked me to help her organise her cluttered home. It took a few weeks to work through every room in her house and we sent loads and loads of unloved and unused stuff to charity. A few weeks later, she called me again and asked me to recommend an interior designer, which I did. The interior designer went through the house and introduced new pieces of furniture, lamps, cushions, bed linen and artwork and—wow—the house really popped!

About ten months later I was running an event and noticed Jane's name on the list. I was excited to see her again, but I was not prepared for the transformation. The everyday, 50-something woman I had previously met had turned into a stunner. She had lost lots of weight, she was wearing a gorgeous outfit and her hair and makeup had been done with style and taste. She looked as though she had just stepped off the catwalk. I was speechless! After recovering my composure, I asked her what the secret to her success was and she replied with words to this effect: 'It's all your fault—you started it! Once my home was organised, I could think again and I could dream again. Then, once it was redecorated, that was the icing on the cake. But I didn't look the part! I was overweight, frumpy and had lost my sparkle and that's what I wanted to get back. So I started a weight-loss and fitness program. Once I lost the weight, I invested in a new wardrobe and used a stylist to create a whole new look for me! But, I could never have done this without taking the first step of releasing the clutter and becoming more organised. You changed my life forever. Thank you.'

Jane's story, and the stories of all my clients, inspired me to write this book, to bring you the system that turned their lives around and triggered a whole chain of new events. I will be with you every step of the way, cheering you on, giving you advice and celebrating your success. I hope just a little bit of your success in life will also be my fault!

Warmest wishes,
MaryAnne Bennie

Introduction

❝Well begun is half done.❞

Aristotle

Regardless of where we live or what we do, we acquire and accumulate items meant to enhance our quality of life. We call these items our possessions, our assets, our things or our stuff. These items come in the form of furniture, clothing, entertainment equipment, tools, cookware, crockery, cutlery, supplies, food, glassware, ornaments, artwork, books, transport, technology, appliances, footwear, paperwork, sports equipment and toys. And that just names a few! When in balance, these items are useful and appreciated: they support us in our endeavours and make life easier and more comfortable.

In an affluent society, people have the means to accumulate more and more. And in this technological age, items become obsolete within a very short time, compelling us to update regularly. Remember the computer you purchased last year? Well, it's a dinosaur today!

These days we have multiples of many items, whereas in days gone by one or none would have been the norm. How many TVs, tennis racquets, mobile phones, computers, salad bowls and kitchen appliances do we really need and, more importantly, do we actually use?

We have an infinite capacity to bring stuff in, but we have a finite capacity to store our stuff. *Everything is competing for space.* Everything needs to earn its right to stay!

Human nature is such that we are reluctant to dispose of something without good reason or without it having a good home to go to, especially if it is in good condition and we paid good money for it. So the accumulation continues...

Homes aren't designed to house large quantities of major appliances and entertainment items. Homes today are designed along minimalist principles, but people are living with the opposite tendencies.

Once our accumulation of possessions exceeds our capacity to store them, we are in big trouble. When something doesn't have a home, it's homeless. Because homeless items have nowhere specific to live, they live anywhere and everywhere. They line the hallways, park on benches, slide under beds, perch on cupboard tops and hide in corners. Then they breed like rabbits! Before we know it we have a house full of mess and the resulting chaos has a detrimental impact on our quality of life.

The statistics are in! A study conducted in 2007 by The Australia Institute found that 88 per cent of Australian homes have at least one cluttered room, with the average home having three or more cluttered rooms. An incredible 59 per cent of women said there was a room in the house they don't like visitors to see and 40 per cent said they felt anxious, guilty or depressed about the clutter in their homes. In 2004 the Australia Institute found that the average Australian household wasted $1226 a year on items purchased but never used. That's a whopping $10.5 billion for the nation. We clearly have a problem.

We are too embarrassed to entertain at home and are constantly frustrated by our attempts to put things in order. No matter what we do, our possessions have outgrown our capacity to store them.

We think more storage will solve the problem so we add cupboards, shelving and containers. Some of us renovate or put on an extension; others relegate the car into the driveway or the street and use the garage as a storage solution. When desperate, we may resort to the 'out-of-sight, out-of-mind' storage technique and rent off-site storage to deal with the excess. If only we had a bigger house, everything would be fine!

Our possessions should support us and our lifestyle. They should reflect our personality and style. They should bring us happiness, not despair. Why, then, do we find the things we took so much pleasure in acquiring are now suffocating us, causing us misery and wasting our precious time?

Sadly, some of the things we acquired on past shopping expeditions no longer have their magnetic appeal. Our love affair is over!

The **in8steps** system helps you to reassess your relationship with your stuff. It shows you how to decide what stays and what goes, and how to efficiently store what remains so it's ready and available when you need it. The delicate balance between your stuff and your available storage is restored. In this new relationship, your stuff will support you now and into the future. But when the time comes to part company, you will know how to gently break the news. The **in8steps** system will show you the way.

Excuses, excuses, excuses

People have many excuses for not getting organised. It's a good idea to look at some common excuses and dismiss them, just in case you are using them to justify your acceptance of the status quo.

Excuse 1: *You think you need everyone in your household to support your organising efforts.* It can be lonely being the organising warrior of the household, but like many crusaders you may have to go it alone. Good leaders lead by example. Organise your own space first and then move into other spaces with respect and permission from adults and the knowledge of children. You never know, they may even decide to join you on your space mission.

Excuse 2: *You think that storage alone will solve your problems.* A good lesson to learn right up front is that it's about you and your relationship with your stuff and rarely about storage. Most homes could do with a bit of extra storage, but the fact is, you will simply continue to fill the storage you have until it's back to overflowing. You need to limit the amount of stuff you keep and then employ the best possible storage solutions. When your stuff and your storage are in harmony, you will be free at last.

Excuse 3: *You think everything you have might come in handy one day.* The truth is that if you did need it, you would most likely not be able to find it in time. If you don't know where something is, you actually don't have it at all. Think about it: how many times have you gone out and purchased something you knew was in your house somewhere? I rest my case! The 80:20 rule says that you use 20 per cent of your stuff 80 per cent of the time—and you use the other 80 per cent irregularly or not at all. Remember that your stuff is competing for space and has to earn the right to stay. Concentrate on making space for the 20 per cent and eliminating as much of the 80 per cent as possible.

Excuse 4: *You believe that sorting and organising takes a lot of time—time that you don't have.* You will actually gain time by having everything sorted and in its place. Sorting does take time because most of your possessions came into your home one item at a time and that's the way they must also be sorted or disposed of.

If you sort your stuff efficiently now, you will save that time many times over when accessing, using and replacing your stuff in the future.

The choice of work pace and time spent sorting is yours. Some people prefer working in short bursts—doing one area at a time—while others like to get the whole room done in one hit.

Ask yourself: Would you rather spend some time organising your stuff once or looking for things over and over and over again?

Excuse 5: *You think that putting things in temporary homes or in safe places will do.* You often say, 'It can go here for now' or 'I'll put it in a safe place'. Both of these storage options are fraught with danger. Temporary and safe storage places are invariably forgotten. Those diamond earrings you put in the pocket of your black jacket may not be found for months or years—or, even worse, be lost forever when you donate the jacket to charity. Now is a good time to dispense with the temporary and safe place options. From now on, everything goes into its correct home and, if it doesn't have a home, one is created.

Excuse 6: *You believe you have been genetically programmed to be disorganised—either in keeping with family tradition or rebelling against it.* I often see people having a bet each way. They are disorganised because they had bad role models. Or, they are disorganised because they had good role models and now they are rebelling and asserting their independence. Both excuses are lame! You're an adult now and able to make your own decisions and choices. So stop falling back on the genetic excuse.

Dismiss all your excuses right now. Help is at hand. The **in8steps** system will bring a huge sigh of relief to anyone wanting to become more organised but not knowing where to start. We will start at the beginning and work step by step through the process until every room in your home is fully organised and you are back in control. So climb on board. Ready or not, here we go!

How to use this book

The best way to use this book is to first read part I and complete all the masterclasses. Armed with this information, go to part II and reorganise the rooms of your home in the order of your choice. I challenge you to do a room a week—you will have your whole house done in next to no time and still have a life! The key is not to bite off more than you can chew. You know how busy your lifestyle is, so work around it and make organising your home a gift to yourself, done at a pace that suits you and in a way that will sustain you now and forever.

> ## Note it!
> Keep a notebook dedicated to your organising project. Use it to take notes, answer questions, record measurements and play around with room plans.

Case studies are provided throughout the book to highlight how real people, just like you, have handled real situations.

Tips for success are sprinkled throughout the book to give you those extra power boosts, that extra edge and those little finishing touches that make a big difference.

Exercises, where you pause to answer questions or make decisions, are placed in strategic locations. Record your responses in your notebook before moving on.

So what are you waiting for? Turn the pages, follow the system and watch your home transform before your very eyes.

PART I

Masterclasses

Part I of this book is critical to your success. This is where I share all of my insider secrets, my technical expertise and my years of experience helping people organise their homes, their offices and their lives.

Masterclass 1: setting up for success gets you in the mood for organising. It's important to have the right frame of mind before you get started on this incredible journey.

Masterclass 2: the in8 steps system takes you through all the ins and outs of the process. You get to understand what each step does, why you do it and how to put them all together.

Masterclass 3: a space mission introduces you to the three elements of space. Understanding the physical, functional and emotional elements of your space will empower you to bring your disorganised home back into balance.

Masterclass 4: getting a handle on hardware is where I reveal my five secret weapons. I've spent years studying shelves, drawers, hanging rods, hooks and containers. I know that may not sound very exciting to you right now, but they are the basis of all storage. By the end of this masterclass, you will love them just as much as I do!

Masterclass 5: time-saving techniques is where I share simple little ideas that you can use every day to make getting organised playful and a lot more fun.

Once you have graduated from the five masterclasses you will be fully qualified and prepared to transform your disorganised and cluttered house into a clean, organised and functional home.

Masterclass 1: setting up for success

> 66Vision without action is merely a dream.
> Action without vision just passes the time.
> Vision with action can change the world!99
>
> *Joel Arthur Barker*

In the mood

Remember the last time you went on a trip? You did some planning, chose a destination, set the dates, decided how to get there, booked your accommodation and set aside some spending money. You really got in the mood. You imagined being in new places, meeting new people and having new experiences. That's how I want you to feel about this trip to your new destination of being organised. I want you to see, feel, smell, hear and taste it. I want the excitement of it to be pulsing through your veins throughout your journey.

Complete the following three exercises to get you in the ultimate organising mood.

Exercise 1: be organised

What does being organised mean to you? Is it having a place for everything and everything in its place? Is it not being embarrassed if someone pops in? Is it having time to do all the things you have been putting on hold all these years?

Visualise it!

Imagine you had a crystal ball and you could see your organised future. What would you see, smell, feel, taste and hear? Take a few moments to visualise and experience your organised future through your crystal ball. Visualise every room in your home in its organised state and ask yourself these questions:

- What do I see?
- How does it smell?
- What can I feel?
- How does it taste?
- What can I hear?

Now close your eyes and answer the questions.

Write your responses for each room in your notebook. You will use your vision for each room in part II.

Tip

Repeat this visualisation exercise whenever you commence organising a room or need a little extra motivation!

Exercise 2: calculate your savings

No time to waste!

How much time and money will you save by being more organised?

You already know that being disorganised costs time and money. But have you ever really thought about how much time and money you will save? Being more organised streamlines every single thing you do: from getting ready in the morning, to going to work, to making dinner, to looking after the house, to retiring in the evening. If you're disorganised, every single thing you do takes more time than necessary. It could be the few extra minutes it takes to move the junk off the ironing board to iron a shirt for work, or the time you waste every day looking for wallets, purses, glasses, remote controls and keys. Maybe it's the 30 minutes you spent on hold on the phone, waiting to explain why you shouldn't have your power cut off, after forgetting to pay the misplaced bill.

Now let's look at your situation and time it.

Tick, tock! Time it!

Calculate your time saving: just think back over the past week and note the time you wasted through being disorganised. The amount of time you wasted will become the amount of time you save.

I will gain _____ hours a week by being more organised. My time savings will come from: _____
_____

Money down the drain!

When it comes to money, just think about the food you waste every week simply because you have no idea what you need when you go shopping. What about the things you buy again because you can't find the ones you already have? If you have ever wasted money on late fees, interest charges and fines for being tardy with your bills, you know how much that hurts. Is your car fading in the sun and losing value due to a disorganised garage? What about other frustrating things such as lost gift vouchers and receipts for warranty items needing repair?

Now let's look at your situation and cost it.

K-ching, k-ching! Cost it!

Calculate your money saving: just think back over the past week and calculate what you lost through being disorganised. The amount of money you lost will become the amount of money you save.

I will save $_____ a week by being more organised. My money savings will come from: _____
_____

Now let's look at your situation and spend it.

Spend it!

You have calculated how much time and how much money you will save by being organised. Now look into the future and imagine how you will spend that time and money.

How will you spend the extra time you have and extra money you save?

_____

_____

Exercise 3: shift your thinking

Talk to yourself!
It's now time to change your mindset.

So often it's the things you say to yourself that keep you from moving forward. This inner conversation is called self-talk. The good thing is that every negative statement you say about yourself or your situation can be turned around to be more positive. Statements such as, 'I've always been disorganised' are not helpful to your success. Instead say, 'I'm learning new organisation skills to achieve my goals'. From now on, focus on the future and forgive the past. Make positive statements every time you slip into negative thinking by changing your self-talk.

Change your mind! One of the self-talk changes you can make is to change from the old idea of 'letting go' to the new concept of 'releasing'. Many people find it hard to 'let go' of their stuff. 'Letting go' assumes a tug of war, with you holding on against an enemy who is pulling your stuff away from you. Well, you don't have to 'let go' of anything. You get to choose what stays and what goes. Your goal is to 'release' items that no longer serve or support you. This simple mindset change frees you to 'release' your things onto the next phase of their journey. It's not all about you. The stuff you 'release' has a higher purpose and a new place to be, serving people who have different needs from you.

Marcia's moving on

Marcia was moving house and she told me something that stuck with me. As she was packing, she asked herself a simple question: 'What things do I want to accompany me into the next phase of my life? What items have earned the right to continue to be in my new space and in my new life?' The items she loved and needed and those from which she received support were packed, while the rest were sent on their own journey elsewhere.

The key is to focus on what you are 'keeping' and not on what you are 'releasing'.

Whether you are moving into a new home or simply reorganising your existing home — affectionately known as 'moving without moving' — the process is the same. From now on you have the opportunity to make a conscious decision about every single item you possess. You have the chance to make a fresh start with a clean slate.

Re-frame it!

Make a list of your negative self-talk statements and turn them into new, positive ones. Here is an example to start you off on a more positive note.

Negative self-talk	Positive self-talk
I don't have time to get organised.	I can break it down and do a little bit at a time.

Now that your mood and confidence have been lifted, you are ready to learn the **in8steps** system. So read on.

The in8steps system

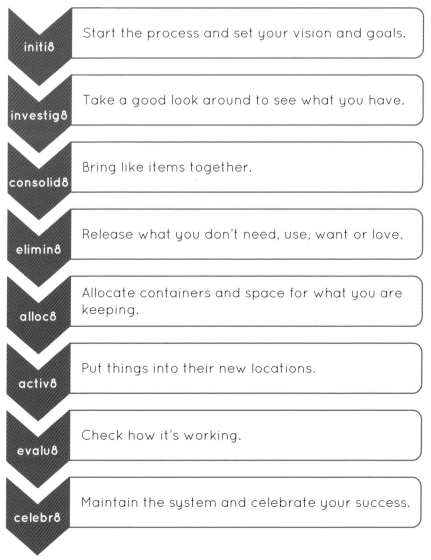

initi8 — Start the process and set your vision and goals.

investig8 — Take a good look around to see what you have.

consolid8 — Bring like items together.

elimin8 — Release what you don't need, use, want or love.

alloc8 — Allocate containers and space for what you are keeping.

activ8 — Put things into their new locations.

evalu8 — Check how it's working.

celebr8 — Maintain the system and celebrate your success.

2

Masterclass 2: the in8steps system

> "Your life is the sum result of all the choices you make, both consciously and unconsciously. If you can control the process of choosing, you can take control of all aspects of your life. You can find the freedom that comes from being in charge of yourself."
>
> *Robert F. Bennett*

Learning the ropes

Remember when you first learned to drive a car? You had to figure out how all the parts of the car worked separately. You practised using the brakes, the accelerator and the steering. You started off having to concentrate on every step, one at a time: 'Put seatbelt on. Start car. Check mirrors. Indicate intentions. Drive forward.' Then, all of a sudden, it all came together and you were driving on a busy street. Learning the **in8steps** system is no different. Once you learn the steps, driving the system will all come together automatically.

Phase it in

The **in8steps** system provides you with easy-to-follow instructions to support you through any organisation project:

 The first two steps are the 'Plan it' phase—for planning and preparation before you begin.

The next four steps are the 'Do it' phase, where the actions of physical sorting and storing are done.

 The final two steps are the 'Review it' phase—for evaluation, maintenance and celebration.

One step at a time

I will show you how to do each step separately, how each phase comes together as a set and how to fast-track the system. So take the time to read through and understand the steps, as your results will be a reflection of how well you follow them.

The in8steps system in a nutshell

Here's a clear breakdown of the three phases and eight steps of the **in8steps** system.

The in8steps system

Plan it	1	initi8	You initiate a plan of attack for your organising project.
	2	investig8	You investigate what you have and how it's working.
Do it	3	consolid8	You consolidate what you have into categories.
	4	elimin8	You eliminate things you no longer use, need, want or love.
	5	alloc8	You allocate space and containers for what you are keeping.
	6	activ8	You activate by preparing space, adjusting storage and placing items into their locations.
Review it	7	evalu8	You evaluate how it looks and works and make adjustments.
	8	celebr8	You celebrate by setting up maintenance and rewarding your success.

The **in8steps** system is common sense, easy to follow and guaranteed to work for your situation. Once you have mastered the theory, you will be ready to put it into practice in any area of your home. So get your notebook out — we're ready to go!

The in8steps system in detail

Let's look at each of the eight steps, one by one.

 Step 1: initi8

The first of the two planning steps is initi8. It will start you on your journey to an organised home. It's like turning on the ignition switch in your head but, as you know, turning on an ignition switch doesn't actually get you moving forward. You need to apply the accelerator and fully commit yourself to the task.

To travel along the correct route you need to identify your frequent frustrations, set your vision and your goals, gather your tools and get in the mood. This won't take long, so hop in the driver's seat and let's get started.

Identify your frequent frustrations

After choosing the room to be organised, you will list everything that frustrates you about it. What annoys you and constantly gets on your nerves? You need to feel the pain in order to appreciate the gain! Get it all down on paper because your frequent frustrations will lead you to your goals. Most of your frequent frustrations will be small things repeated over and over again. So make sure you list things such as running out of underwear, finding wet towels on the bed, jumbling through the entire plastics drawer and not finding what you want, tripping over toys or not knowing what's for dinner at night.

Set your vision and your goals

Keeping your frequent frustrations in mind, write your vision and your goals for each room. Remember: you will be measuring your success against the vision and the goals you set. In your vision and goals statement make sure you include what you want to achieve, an estimated budget, your timeline and a reward for completion.

Pamela's pantry plan

Pamela's simple vision and goals statement for her pantry was 'My pantry is filled with fresh, nutritious food for my family. Extra shelves have been installed to reduce space wastage and I now have a great system for managing my spices. I have two drawers filled with see-through containers holding all the staples I use every day. Everything is labelled and easy to remove, use and replace. I am allowing all day Tuesday and $500 to get it right. Once it's finished I'll treat myself to a massage and a facial'.

Gather your tools

You'll need to assemble an organising kit, a tool kit and a cleaning kit to assist you in this process.

The organising kit is everything you need in order to do your sorting. In particular, you will be using a number of temporary sorting containers during the process. Make do with what is available around the home such as cardboard boxes, shoe boxes, plastic containers of all sizes, bowls, cups, buckets, trays and so on. You should also collect empty boxes from the local supermarket or liquor store. A container is simply a receptacle or an area for gathering like items together. Tabletops, bench surfaces, floors and tops of beds should also be used for sorting. So you might place all your glassware onto a table or benchtop when sorting the kitchen, or place stacks of clothing onto the bed as you tackle the wardrobe. The organising kit also contains your notebook and pen, a camera and your sorting accessories.

The tool kit is essential for when you need to tighten a screw, adjust a shelf or repair a hinge. Keep it handy and in a designated spot (for example, just outside the door of the room you are working in). Most likely you already have a tool kit in the garage or workshop.

The cleaning kit will be used to spot clean along the way and to thoroughly clean storage surfaces before replacing your sorted items. It is easily made up with items you have in the house.

Your kits

Organising kit	Tool kit	Cleaning kit
Notebook and pen	Tape measure	Duster
'Bin it', 'Gift it', 'Sell it', 'Move it' containers	Hammer	Bucket with clean soapy water
Range of sorting containers	Screwdrivers	Sponges
Masking tape and marking pen	Pliers	Cleaning cloths
Label maker and tape	Spanners	Gloves
Garbage bags	Scissors	Apron
Zip-lock bags	Step ladder	Floor cleaners
Rubber bands	Packing Tape	Dust mask
Timer	Drill	Cleaning sprays
Camera	Extension cords	Surface protection cloths

Get in the mood

Before you begin organising, get into the right frame of mind for the task ahead. Here are several suggestions for keeping you focused and on track:

- Work with music playing, turn it up and move to the beat!
- Have lots of water and a few healthy snacks on hand.
- Divert your phones to message bank. This is no time to take calls.
- Turn your TV and computer off—emails can wait.
- Get the family out of the house unless they are actively involved in what you are doing.
- Dress for success. Wear comfortable clothes and shoes.

 Step 2: investig8

The second planning step is investig8 and your role is to look at your room from an objective perspective, as though seeing it for the very first time.

Before you tackle any room, take a few minutes to look around and assess the space. Doing this now will save you making annoying mistakes later, such as finding that you have placed something

Is this one of your frequent frustrations?

needing power too far away from a power point. Or having glare from a window shining onto your computer screen. Or finding you have placed things in the wrong location. During the investig8 step you should do five quick things:

- *Carry out an overview.* Note the physical, functional and emotional elements of the room. Put simply, physical covers all the tangible items in the room, functional covers all the tasks performed in the room and emotional is all about how the room makes you feel. These three space elements are covered in detail in masterclass 3 and are also elaborated on for each room in part II.

- *Measure up.* If you feel you need to play around with the furniture and storage components, draw a floor plan and take measurements as necessary. Not all rooms will require alteration, but be ready to make any changes that will address your frequent frustrations and achieve your vision and your goals. In particular, you may need to measure shelves and drawers to work out the best possible storage solutions.

- *Take unhappy snaps.* Take photos of each room and the insides of cupboards and drawers. Be careful—items sometimes have a habit of tumbling out when you least expect it! These 'before' photos will be fascinating to look back on once your organising is complete and they will also motivate you to stay on track.

- *Complete a discovery tour.* Look in every cupboard, drawer, nook and cranny to see what is stored there. You will discover lots of interesting stuff during your inspection, so be prepared to hear yourself repeating, 'Oh, that's where it is!' every time you discover some long lost item from your 'Where did I put it?' list. This inspection gives you a good idea of which items are stored where and it will be invaluable when you begin sorting your stuff into categories later on. It also reveals storage potential because you will discover that some cupboards and drawers are mainly filled with junk. All of a sudden, after ditching the junk, you will have bonus storage you didn't know about.

- *Fix anything that needs fixing.* Note anything you need to purchase or fix in your notebook. You may notice hanging hinges, loose handles, dripping taps, wonky drawers, blown light bulbs or sagging shelves. By noting them now, you can quickly rectify problems yourself or have plenty of time to call in professional help if required.

Your two planning and preparation steps are now complete and it's time to get into action.

Step 3: consolid8

Consolid8 is the first of the four action steps. These action steps—consolid8, elimin8, alloc8 and activ8—work together as a team, so as soon you begin consolidating a category—for example, 'linen'—you begin to involve the next three steps. This will become obvious as you read on.

Big fat categories

The consolid8 step shows you how to sort your stuff into big fat categories without turning the house upside down. A 'big fat category' is a broad category used to group a collection of like items together. The broadness of the category depends on the quantity, disarray and variety of what you are sorting. Big fat categories can easily be sorted into subcategories. For example, the big fat category of 'linen' can be sorted into the subcategories of sheets, towels, pillowcases, tea towels, tablecloths and so on. Common big fat categories and their subcategories are detailed for each room in part II.

The fab four

Eliminating stuff is the holy grail of organising! To get a room organised it's essential that we reduce the amount of stuff in it, and there are four ways of achieving this. You can 'Bin it', 'Gift it', 'Sell it' or 'Move it'.

You will need four rigid containers to house these categories. Put a label on each container and they are ready to accompany you on your organising mission. Take them with you on every organising job and try to fill them as much as possible! Here's what you fill them with:

The fab four and friends

- The 'Bin it' container is for obvious rubbish, including rubbish for recycling, and for unwanted items of no commercial value or use to anyone else.
- The 'Gift it' container is for stuff you no longer want but which is of some commercial value and is of use to someone else. You can gift it to family, friends or charity.
- The 'Sell it' container is for stuff you no longer want, but which has significant commercial value. It can be sold online or in a garage or yard sale. Of course, if you don't plan to sell your unwanted stuff you won't need this container.
- The 'Move it' container is for stuff you still want, but which does not belong in this room. Place items you plan to repair into this container as well.

Many items will go instinctively into these four containers during the consolidate step. As you can see, you are already integrating the elimin8 step into this earlier consolid8 step.

Tip

Label all your sorting containers using masking tape, which can be easily removed later but won't fall off like sticky notes or pieces of paper.

Sally sorts her baby's room

Sally gives her old — but good — baby clothes, toys and equipment to her sister Rebecca and recycles the rest. She doesn't have the time or energy to sell her stuff so she doesn't need a 'Sell it' bin. So when sorting the baby's room, she grabs some cardboard boxes and first creates a 'Rebecca' box and a 'recycle' box. Her grandmother does all her clothing repairs and so the 'Nana' box is born. As the boxes fill — or at the end of her organising — she places them into her car, ready to be delivered to their relevant destinations.

Remember that what you call your containers needs to make sense to you. Sally's made perfect sense to her.

Don't mess it up

When organising a room, you are faced with the prospect of making a huge mess in the process. The last thing you should do is take everything out at once—you simply won't have anywhere to put it all. And if you had to stop for any reason, you would be in a worse mess than you were to start with!

Steady as you go

Take it easy, work systematically and tackle one area or one category at a time, to keep the task manageable. For example, in the kitchen you could tackle the 'pantry' as an area or

What not to do!

'pots and pans' as a category. The pantry could be subcategorised into cans, cereals, dry goods, crackers and biscuits, spices, sauces and so on. The 'pots and pans' could be put into the subcategories of frypans, small pots, medium pots and large pots.

Work with what you have

Big fat categories are a starting point designed to bring like items together so you can deal with them as a group. This keeps the number of sorting containers you need to start with to a minimum. If, however, you are only sorting your linen cupboard, then everything in the cupboard is already sorted into the big fat category of 'linen'. You would immediately sort into subcategories such as towels, tea towels, beach towels, sheets, tablecloths and so on. Most of your storage will already be somewhat sorted into categories, so use this to your advantage. You can also rearrange things within the storage instead of taking everything out. You will still need sorting containers to consolidate items that don't belong. While you are doing this, you are also eliminating unwanted items to the 'Bin it', 'Gift it', 'Sell it' and 'Move it' containers.

Disaster zone!

If you have a room that is a total disaster, where stuff is piled and spread haphazardly around the room, you will need to create the biggest, fattest categories you can. For example, 'clothing' would be placed into one container (or one corner of the room), 'toys and games' into another, 'reading material' into another and so on. These would then be broken down into subcategories once the first sort has been completed. The four constant categories—'Bin it', 'Gift it', 'Sell it' and 'Move it'—will have significantly reduced the amount of stuff remaining, making it much easier to sort each big fat category into its subcategories one at a time.

Worst first

If you are working in a room that already has most of its contents stored in reasonable categories, work with these categories and areas last. First, tackle the areas that are in disarray (such as the junk cupboard) using big fat categories to group like items together. Once the junk cupboard is empty, place as many as you can of your big fat category containers back into the cupboard to get them out of the way temporarily. Now choose the next area to sort and integrate items into the existing big fat categories in the cupboard and create new ones as necessary. As soon as you know one big fat category is complete, you can move that category on to the next step: elimin8.

Some order please!

The sequence in which you sort your categories will often be self-determining. When you take items out of one location, sometimes they are returned to the same spot, while at other times they are best stored elsewhere. In order to store them elsewhere, you need to remove the things that are already there. So whatever was stored there determines the next area and categories you tackle. And so it continues. If items are put back in the same location, you get to choose the next area and categories you want to organise.

Kate's corner conquered

When Kate was organising her pots and pans, she removed them from their drawers and eliminated those she no longer wanted. After considering all her space, she decided she wanted to use the corner cupboard for her pots and pans, but it was overflowing with an assortment of plastic containers. As her plastic containers were already in their big fat 'plastic containers' category, she decided to take them straight to her sorting table where she first matched all the lids with the bases and tossed the leftover lids. She decided that she would only keep the plastic containers that stacked easily and neatly together and tossed those that did not meet her criteria. Now she could see what she had left. She placed them into two containers and decided to store them on a shelf of another cupboard. But this was full of cookbooks, which became the next category she had to deal with. And so it continued.

Fast forward!

Within a short time you will have consolidated all your categories and broken them down into subcategories, and maybe for the first time you will see just how much you have. The consolid8 step leads directly into the elimin8 step. Remember: you don't have to have consolidated everything to move to this step. As soon as you are pretty sure you have any category fully consolidated into subcategories, you can move forward to the next step and start eliminating.

Corner conquered!

 ## Step 4: elimin8

Elimin8 is the second of the four action steps. This step finally and completely gets rid of what you don't use, need, want or love and sets some limits for the future. To proceed to this step you must have at least one category fully sorted into its subcategories. For example, 'linen' will have been sorted into towels, tea towels, beach towels and so on. Much of what you started with has already been discarded along the way because they were easy decisions. If you have linen stored in other areas of the house, collect it now and sort it into the subcategories as well. You can now see exactly how much of each subcategory you have, and how much space it will need. This is very valuable information and it may be the first time you have seen all these items together in the one place. You may be shocked by the amount you see!

Right size?

If you are really serious about getting organised, it is essential that you reduce the amount of stuff you keep to the things you use, need, want or love. Do you remember the 80:20 rule? A whopping 80 per cent of your stuff is used irregularly or not at all! Your aim is not to downsize for downsizing's sake, but to 'right size' for your current and future needs.

It's crunch time

Do a final sort of your subcategories to see what can go into the 'Bin it', 'Gift it', 'Sell it' or 'Move it' containers—and be ruthless! If you are having difficulty deciding, you are not alone. Everyone struggles to some extent with releasing some items. When in serious doubt, place the item into a container labelled 'Not sure' and keep moving through your subcategories. Finally, go back to your 'Not sure' container and ask yourself the following questions while holding each item:

- Do I use you? If so, how often? When was the last time? When will be the next time?
- Do I need you? Could I use something else as a substitute or borrow you?
- Do I really want you or just the memory of you or where you came from? If you just want the memory, take a photo!
- Do I love you? Are you of sufficient sentimental value for me to keep?

From the answers you give to these four questions, you will know whether to keep or to release the item.

Home shopping—your household supermarket

Create a family household supermarket for extra supplies of commonly used items. This secondary storage space can be in the garage, in a hall cupboard or in the laundry. Store extra toilet paper, tissues, shampoo, toothpaste, soap, washing detergent, sponges and those items you are lucky enough to buy at special prices. Whenever you run out of these in primary storage, go shopping in your household supermarket. Having a household supermarket reduces the stress on your primary storage space.

Only love knows no boundaries

Set some limits. How much of any category do you really need? How much is enough? Well, if you want to retain your sanity, what you keep is largely governed by the amount of storage space you have. If you don't want to be smothered by your stuff, you must set some limits. Remember: you have infinite capacity to bring things in but only finite capacity to store them. So let's talk about setting those limits. Setting limits is asking yourself what is a reasonable amount of any one item or category for you to have, given your family size, your lifestyle and your storage capacity. Once you set your limits, your limits will set you free.

There are three ways to set your limits: by number, by storage space or by date. Let's look at each in a bit more detail.

- *Limit by number.* Limiting by number is simply deciding on the number of items to keep in both primary and secondary storage. You may decide on 10 as a reasonable number of business shirts, or four as a reasonable number of frypans, or two bath towels per family member, plus an extra four for emergencies or guests. At the same time, limit the number you have in secondary storage. For example, 12 rolls of toilet paper, 10 cans of tomatoes or four bottles of shampoo. The choice is yours, but it will be made easier when you can actually see how many of these items you currently have. And—guess what—they are now sitting right in front of you in their sorted subcategories!

- *Limit by storage space.* Limiting by storage space means you limit by the amount of space you are prepared to dedicate to the items or category. One bookcase may be the storage space you decide on to store your books, or one drawer to store your socks, or one shelf of the pantry to store your canned food. You will have these items in front of you and will be able to see the space they currently take up. Are you willing to devote that much space to them in your allocated area?

- *Limit by date.* Limiting by date means using a date or a time frame when setting your limits. You may decide on keeping the latest 12 months of a car magazine, or the last 12 months of electricity accounts, or to keep tax deductible receipts for five years to comply with taxation requirements. It will be easy for you to set these date limits with the items sitting in front of you sorted into date order.

Whichever method you use, setting limits is a mindset and is essential for balancing your storage space and your stuff.

What's the bag limit?

Think back to the last time you flew to a holiday destination. Do you remember your flight? Do you remember the baggage limit you were set? Did you manage to have a great holiday with only 20 kilograms of baggage? Can you imagine how much you would have taken if there were no limits? The airline limit meant that you had to evaluate your baggage and only take the items that were necessary. Get the picture? Now you need to do this with your home. Only keep the items you use, need, want or love, and release the rest.

Hit the road, Jack!

Dispose of it! It's time for your clutter to leave the building or move to another room. The 'Bin it' items can be tossed into the rubbish and recycling bins. The 'Gift it' items can be given to family, friends or a charity. The 'Sell it' items can be stored somewhere until you have enough to warrant a garage or yard sale, or you can immediately put them up for sale online. The 'Move it' items get moved to their correct rooms or secondary storage areas, while items for repair go to the relevant repair area or person. It's important that everything leaves the scene of the crime as soon as humanly possible!

Step 5: alloc8

Alloc8 is the third of the four action steps. In this step you allocate the most appropriate containers and the best possible locations for the things you use, need, want or love. Before reaching this step, you will have already decided what you are keeping in one or more categories.

Shopping time

You should now be able to see what you need to store and whether the existing storage is adequate or can be modified to suit. If the current storage is not adequate, now is the time to decide what you need to purchase to house it efficiently. It's important not to make these storage decisions until you reach this step. I've seen so many people go out and purchase containers, shelves and cupboards, and even hire external storage before they have reached this stage, only to find they haven't chosen the right type or amount for their needs. Please, please wait until this step to decide on storage adjustments and to make purchasing decisions. Now that you have decluttered your stuff, you'll most likely find you have sufficient space that requires just a few modifications. Before you go shopping for any new storage components, re-check all measurements. Remember the golden rule: measure twice, shop once!

Value your space

Not all space is the same. Like real estate, some areas are valued higher than others. Your space is no different. Generally, the areas that are easiest to get to, such as the fronts of shelves and areas within arm's reach of seated or standing positions, are considered to be primary storage areas. Backs of cupboards, high spaces and low spaces, under beds, and areas external to the house are considered to be secondary storage areas of the home. You need to know the difference and to convert as much secondary storage space to primary storage space as you can. Things you use infrequently and items surplus to your current needs belong in secondary storage space.

Your move

The key determinants to where you place items are based on how often you use them, their shape, size, weight and the overall category size. In addition, you need to take into account the room you have to work with and its configuration. The goal is to optimise your storage and make things as accessible as you can, in the least possible number of moves. My personal measure of success is that I can remove or replace anything in my home within two moves. You should aim to do the same.

In masterclass 4 you will learn all about storage options and how to make the most of your space. In part II of the book, you will be given loads of specific tips on storage options for every room of your home. Right now, it's enough to know that after you have eliminated everything you no longer use, need, want or love, you will place what you are keeping into the most appropriate containers and storage.

 ## Step 6: activ8

Activ8 is the last of the four action steps. Roll up your sleeves because it's now time to get to work and reap the rewards of the consolidation, elimination and allocation steps. With the help of your tool kit, other members of the family or professionals, make any required adjust-ments to existing storage and install the new storage components you have purchased.

Spring clean
Give all storage areas a good spring clean. Some items will need to be dusted or cleaned before they are placed into their new clean storage locations.

Put it away
You can now go about putting all your stuff in its place. Like all the other action steps, the activ8 step can also be done in stages. It depends on the size of the room, the amount of stuff and the time you have available. Now is the time to label containers, shelves and drawers with their contents. Once everything is put away, finish off the spring clean by doing the floors, light fittings and windows.

 ## Step 7: evalu8

Evalu8 is the first of the two review steps. In this step you need to evaluate your system to see how it's working. Get your notebook out and go back to the notes you took during the 'Plan it' phase to make sure you have addressed all the issues you had with this room. Have you achieved your vision and your goals? Is the space physically, functionally and emotionally working for you? Are you easily able to locate, retrieve, use and replace every item you have deemed necessary to your lifestyle? Do you feel you have put your own personality into this room? Have you installed a system that has eliminated your frequent frustrations? Have you disposed of everything that needed to go? How do you feel now? In your notebook write a few notes on what you have achieved, how you did it and any improvements you can make in the next room to be organised.

Happy snaps

Now get your camera out and take your 'after' photos. Then compare them to your 'before' photos. What a difference! Can you believe it? It's done—and if you can do this room you can do the entire house. The **in8steps** system will be with you all the way.

Life is a journey

If you're happy with the result, leave it alone. If you've discovered anything that still isn't right, make some adjustments. Remember that things change! Babies are born, relationships change, children leave home and we change our jobs, our hobbies and our interests. Your stuff and your space will need to change in tandem with the changes in your life. The **in8steps** system can easily adapt to your evolving lifestyle, so continue to evaluate this room periodically and make the necessary changes.

 Step 8: celebr8

Celebr8 is the second of the two review steps. In this step you should have the champagne on ice because you are almost done. You have achieved your vision and your goals. You have a room that is clean, organised and functional.

An ounce of prevention

> I hate housework! You make the beds, you do the dishes—and six months later you have to start all over again.
>
> *Joan Rivers*

Now is the time to take preventative measures to keep the room in check. There are tasks that must be done regularly. Create a home care schedule to manage regular home cleaning and maintenance. This will keep your home humming!

Timely tasks: specialise

There are various things that you do over and over again in every room of your home. In the laundry you have clothing to wash, dry and iron. In the bedrooms you have beds to make and sheets to change. In the bathrooms you have towels to change and supplies to top up. In the kitchen you have meals to make and dishes to wash, dry and put away. And in the office you have paperwork to complete. These actions are room specific.

Timely tasks: generalise

In addition to room-specific tasks, there are various regular general cleaning actions such as dusting, cleaning, vacuuming and floor washing to be done, usually on a weekly basis. Other regular maintenance actions such as cleaning windows, light fittings and soft furnishings are usually done monthly or quarterly. These actions are general and apply to all rooms.

Home care schedule

Set up your home care schedule in just three steps.

- List all the jobs that need to be done to keep your home clean, organised and functional.
- Add how often each job needs to be done—daily, weekly, monthly and so on.
- Create your home care schedule for cleaning and maintenance.

Your home care schedule will look something like this.

Example of a home care schedule

Daily	Weekly	Monthly	Quarterly
Make beds	Change sheets	Wash doona covers	Rotate mattresses
Hang up clothes	Empty waste paper baskets	Vacuum soft furnishings	Wash mattress and pillow protectors
Wash, dry and iron clothes	Vacuum carpets and wash floors	Clean blinds	Clean windows
Empty kitchen bin	Dust furniture	Clean oven	Tidy pantry

Once you have created your home care schedule, be sure to:

- *lock it in.* Once you have listed the tasks and their frequency you just need to lock in times to do them. You can outsource jobs to other family members or to professionals, but the tasks need to be done by someone.

- *raise the bar.* In masterclass 5 you'll learn how to set rules and how to create rituals. Now is the time to apply these time-saving techniques. Once you have organised your home you will set new standards, new rules and new rituals to keep your home clean, organised and functional.

- *maintain it.* Your home care schedule is the backbone and lifeblood of your system. When you start from an organised base, you can forget about cleaning for hours and hours. Everything you do will take less time and energy than it used to.

Congratulations! It's time to celebrate. You did it!

Pop the cork!

It's time to collect your reward—and you have certainly earned it. On your journey you have created a well-organised home or room that you can be proud of. In the future you will enjoy the benefits of your work over and over again. You will be happy to share the results with your family and friends.

Putting it all together

Now you are familiar with all the steps in the **in8steps** system. You can see that while they follow a sequence, you can combine steps and fast-track whenever you like. You may be organising your children's wardrobe and right away you know you will need to raise the hanging rods and add a few extra shelves. Even though that is step 6, you are onto it already. You may also know which containers will best fit in the shelves, or which coathangers you prefer. So go ahead and purchase them sooner rather than later. You might already have an effective home care schedule that you use to clean the house, so you don't need to reinvent it. You will know what to do and how best to adapt the **in8steps** system to your own home, your lifestyle and your work preferences. Remember: it's just like driving a car—once you get the hang of it, it becomes automatic.

Now move on to masterclass 3: a space mission, where you will learn about the three elements of space.

3

Masterclass 3: a space mission

"A good home must be made, not bought."

Joyce Maynard

The three elements of space

Have you ever walked into a room and felt there was something wrong? You couldn't quite put your finger on it, but it didn't feel right. Chances are that one of the three elements of space was out of balance.

The three elements of space are:

- physical
- functional
- emotional.

When one or more element is out of balance, the room lacks something. That something can be fixed by finding which of the elements isn't working. By examining each of the elements you will be able to identify what's wrong with the room and correct it. Sometimes it's just a minor adjustment and at other times it requires a bit of rearranging of furniture and the introduction or removal of items to balance the space.

Let's get physical

All rooms have dimensions, layout, proportions, colour, lighting, aspects, views, temperature, storage capacity, furniture, accessories, fixtures and fittings, and a whole lot more. These are physical elements. If a room is too dark, or too hot, or has way too much in it for its size, or doesn't have enough storage, it needs to be reorganised.

Physical elements include:

- The size of the space and of the items within the space.
- The actual items in the space. Note style, age, shape, configuration, versatility and state of repair.
- The positioning within the space. Note locations of doors, power points, windows, heating ducts, return-air vents and cooling systems. Note the layout of the room and be aware of what is fixed and what is movable.
- The lighting in the space. Note the amount of natural and artificial lighting, window coverings and aspect of the room (whether it is facing north, south, east or west). Consider the natural lighting in different seasons as the lighting changes significantly season by season.
- The temperature, including heating and cooling of the space.
- The colours within the space.
- The capacity of the space. Note the quantities and type of stuff stored in the space and the amount of storage available.

Once you identify problematic physical elements, you can fix them. Sometimes it's the simple things—such as adding a few power points or a lamp, or moving a piece of furniture out of the room—that make a big difference.

Let's get functional

Every room has functions performed in it. Meals are cooked, TV is watched, people sleep, assignments are completed, books are read and written, laundry is washed, people bathe and cars are parked. If functions are performed with ease, the room can be called functional. If functions are difficult to perform, then the room is dysfunctional and needs to be reorganised or tweaked.

Functional elements include:

- The tasks that are performed in the space.
- The systems, processes, flows and routines undertaken in the space. Clutter zones are just bottlenecks in the system. They are evidence that there is a functional malfunction.

- The tools and equipment used to perform the functions of life and the instructions that assist with the functions. An oven and a computer are physical elements in a room, but if you don't have the instructions to make them work, they are not functional.
- The names used to describe the space. The names we give to rooms and spaces sometimes dictate how we treat them. Names, such as kitchen, bedroom, junk room, spare room, junk drawer, landing and storage shed, all elicit meanings and attract items. What do you put in your junk drawer or on the landing?
- The labels attached to items and files. Labels declare to everyone an intention to keep things in order. They are used on containers to let people know about their contents and save time and energy by quickly and easily leading us to what we want.
- The access to the space. Is it too high, too low, at eye level, at waist level or is it an awkward corner?
- The users of the space. Who uses the space and how is it used? Kitchens, for example, have many users, and adults and children see the space very differently. Safety and access are very important. Children need to be able to reach items they need, but not the poisons or medications. Adults like to have everyday items within arm's reach. The aged or disabled may need extra devices to improve a room's functionality.

Tip

A good test of functionality is to check whether you can remove, use and replace an item within one or two movements. If you can't, it's time for some reorganisation.

Let's get emotional

Rooms elicit feelings too! Go to the doorway of any room in your home and ask yourself how this room makes you feel. Some answers I have heard include happy, calm, confused, depressed, overwhelmed and sad. Emotions can be lifted by adding items such as photos, artwork, flowers, music, candles, soft furnishings, colour and sentimental items to a room.

Your rooms should express your personality and give you positive emotional responses. The photo below shows a section of a living room in physical, functional and emotional harmony.

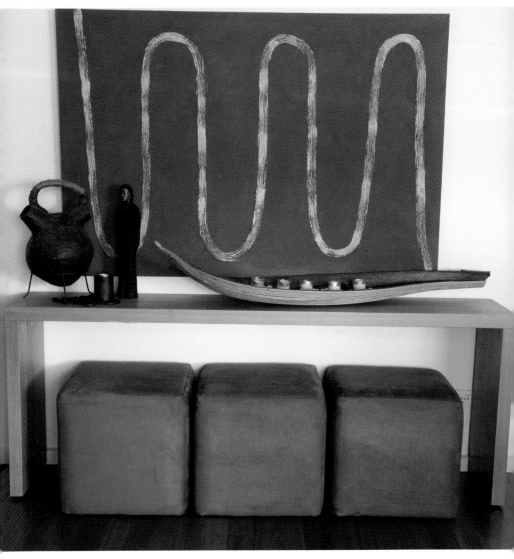

Physical, functional and emotional elements of a room

The table physically displays decorative pieces but functionally doubles as a serving table. Ottomans, used for extra seating or as side tables, are stored neatly underneath. The art and ornamental pieces have personal relevance to the owners and provide emotional support. The tea light candles can be lit to change the ambience and mood of the room when entertaining.

Emotional elements include all of the *feelings* evoked by the space, including:

- warm or cool feelings
- welcoming or unwelcoming feelings
- calm or chaotic feelings
- personal feelings such as confidence, control, empowerment, authenticity, comfort and freedom.

Use your knowledge of the three elements of space to bring every room in your home back into harmony. Refer to this masterclass whenever you feel one of your rooms doesn't feel right and pinpoint the problem.

Mission accomplished! Now move on to masterclass 4: getting a handle on hardware, where I will reveal my five secret weapons for organising your home.

4

Masterclass 4: getting a handle on hardware

A friend is the only person you will let into the house when you are 'turning out drawers'.

Pam Brown

Some storage secrets

Most people embark on their organising journey without a clue about storage hardware. You won't be making this mistake. Instead, you'll arm yourself with some insider secrets, so you'll know exactly what will and what won't work in any storage situation. You'll learn about the little idiosyncrasies of shelves, drawers, hanging rods, hooks and containers. By understanding the components that make up a space, you'll make informed choices about what to do, instead of running off to the shops and coming back with storage hardware you don't need.

Please wait!

One of the keys to organising is that you organise first and shop *last*. You can make do with what you have until you know what you really need. You don't know what you really need until you have sorted through your stuff. So remember, shopping happens *last*.

Arm yourself

Did you know that your storage hardware arsenal is made up of only five basic components? So it makes sense to understand how they work, what they can do and how to put them together to form the best possible storage solutions in your home. They are your secret weapons!

Secret weapon 1: shelves

A shelf is a shelf, is a shelf, is a shelf... No it isn't! Shelves have great strengths but they also have limitations. By understanding how they work, you can implement solutions to overcome any weaknesses in your existing or future shelving.

Delving into shelving

Shelves are mostly made from melamine, timber, glass, plastic or wire. Choose a material to suit your storage needs and situation. Use waterproof shelving in wet areas, timber or glass in living rooms, or cabinets and melamine in the pantry.

Width, depth and thickness

The width, depth and thickness of a shelf can affect its strength:

- The wider the shelf, the weaker it becomes, so limit the weight it carries.
- If overloaded, a shelf may bow in the middle and eventually collapse.
- Distribute weight along a shelf, keeping heavier items towards the supported ends.
- You can reinforce a shelf with extra shelf pins or batons to strengthen it.
- Glue two shelves together to provide additional strength.
- To stop the shelves bowing, try turning them over occasionally if they're reversible.

The size of a shelf can affect how practical it is to store items:

- If shelves are to be used to store folded clothing or linen, aim for widths in multiples of 300 mm.
- Shelves of 300 mm, 600 mm, 900 mm and 1200 mm widths enable neat stacks of folded items to be stored with no wastage of space.
- A 500 mm shelf is too wide for most folded items and isn't wide enough for two stacks side by side.

The 'same: same' technique

Deep shelves always seem to hide stuff at the back, making access difficult. You have to remove everything to find the item you need. But there is a solution to this problem and I like to call it the 'same: same' technique. You simply use two identical containers, each half

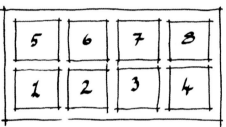

'Same: same' in action

the size of the depth of the shelf, and place one in the front and one in the back. In order to get to the back storage area, you only have to remove one item—the front container. You can use this technique with most types of containers, boxes or magazine boxes. Place items you use less frequently in the rear position. Then label the shelf or the front container to indicate what's stored in front and what's stored behind. Of course, label the rear container as well. Alternatively, you can stick a cupboard storage guide on the inside of the cupboard door to indicate where items are stored.

The 'same: same' technique works well in many situations:

- Have folded bath towels in the front and back layer of a shelf.
- Have household bath towels in the front and guest towels or beach towels in the back.
- For seasonal clothing, for example, put winter clothing behind and summer clothing in front.

- In a pantry you could have older stock in the front and fresher reserve stock behind it.
- With files, put last year's folders in the back, with the current year's folders in the front.

The 'many: few' technique

The back of deep shelves can also be used effectively by placing a row of items vertically at the back, followed by a few boxes of items at the front. I like to call it the 'many: few' technique: 'many' in the back with 'few' in the front. In order to get to the back storage area,

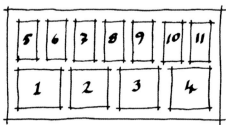

'Many: few' in action

you only have to remove one or two items in the front. Place items you use less frequently in the rear position. Then label the shelf or the front containers to indicate what's stored in front and what's stored behind. Alternatively, you can stick a cupboard storage guide on the inside of the cupboard door showing where items are stored.

The 'many: few' technique works well in many situations:

- Have sets of party glasses (the many) at the back of a deep cupboard, with a couple of containers in the front (the few).
- In your laundry cupboard, have a row of vases at the back of a deep cupboard, with a few stacks of towels in front of them.
- In a children's room, place a row of books at the rear of a deep cupboard, with a few boxes of toys in front of them.
- In a deep bookcase, place a row of novels at the back and a few stacks of books in front. Remove one stack to reveal the titles of the novels.

Fixed and adjustable shelves

Fixed shelves are set in place and cannot be moved. Adjustable shelves can easily be moved, removed or added. The position of adjustable shelves depends on the drilled holes available. You can always drill extra holes to make them even more versatile or to add an extra shelf between your fixed shelves. The number of shelves you need in a cupboard or unit depends on what you're storing, but as a general rule plan for more shelves rather than fewer. Most cupboards can use at least one extra shelf.

Reach the heights

When organising shelving that's above eye level, it's always best to store tall, light items on the top shelf. This makes the items on this shelf easier to reach, enabling you to access them without needing a stepladder. For instance, the top shelf of a pantry could have two or three tall containers holding spare cereal, crackers, napkins, packs of sauces or soups, paper plates or any other lightweight items. In another cupboard, the top shelf could have a container with the attachments for your appliances while another tall container may hold baking tinware such as trays, cake tins and muffin pans all standing up on their sides.

The low down

For shelving units that go down to floor level, store tall and heavy items on the lowest shelf. Place them into containers that are easy to slide out. If the floor is the bottom shelf, as in a walk-in pantry or wardrobe, use containers on castors on the floor (under the lowest shelf) so they can be rolled out when needed or for cleaning.

Close the gap

To best utilise your shelving, you want as little unused space as possible between the shelves. This is why adjustable shelves are ideal. Store items of roughly the same height on a shelf, as a combination of tall and low items creates pockets of unused space. You can create uniformity by using a row of identical-height containers and work to that height.

Behind closed doors

If you have a set of shelves behind cupboard doors, consider using the back of the doors as storage to hang things from. To do this you have to be sure the hung items fit when the doors are closed. If you need a bit more room, remove the shelves and cut a bit off the back to create the gap you need at the front. This is ideal for spice racks on the doors of pantries or jewellery holders on the backs of wardrobe doors.

Irregular shelves

Irregular shelves are not standard in shape or style. They may be corner shelves, cut-away shelves in pantries or custom-made shelves in tricky spaces.

Stepping up

Step shelves are shelves with side supports and are used to create extra layers of storage in certain situations—such as in corner cupboards or when the space is really wide and a regular shelf can't be installed easily. Step shelves are great because they are portable, so you can move them around whenever you like. They are very easy to make and can be made to any size to suit your needs.

Cornered

Corner cupboards have deep recesses that are very difficult to access. Due to their shape, shelves in corner cupboards generally need to be fitted at the time of construction and are difficult, if not impossible, to install or remove afterwards.

A clever way to deal with corner cupboards is to use a number of identical containers of a depth and height slightly smaller than the depth and height of the shelves in the corner cupboard. Place the containers along one back wall of the cupboard so that the container closest to the door opening slides out easily and freely. Then place another container or two against the other back wall, with at least one of them able to slide forward freely through the other door opening. That way, to access anything in the cupboard you only need to move a container or two. Store infrequently used items, such as Christmas tableware or picnic items, in deep corners, and plastic containers, plastic tableware or baking pans in the containers closest to the door. There are also purpose-built solutions available—such as lazy Susans—to solve your corner cupboard problems.

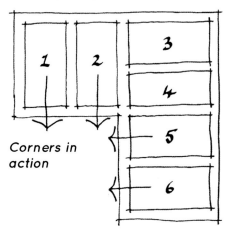

Corners in action

Corner cupboards can work brilliantly for pots and pans. Place pots and pans, complete with lids, onto shelves with handles facing forward. Add a shallow shelf at the top to accommodate your frypans.

Roll on

Roll-out shelves are really just drawers. However, as they are called 'roll-out shelves' they are

A lazy Susan can be a great corner-cupboard option

mentioned here. These are shelves that roll out on runners—like drawers—but are hidden behind cupboard doors. They often replace shelves in under-bench storage, particularly in kitchens. They are ideal for storing crockery, everyday glassware, salad bowls, bakeware, and pots and pans.

Secret weapon 2: drawers

Drawers are by far everyone's favourite storage component because they hide a multitude of sins and create the illusion that everything is neat and tidy.

Win, lose or drawer?

Where would we be without drawers? By simply pulling on a handle you can make their contents come out to greet you. With a gentle push it all goes away, out of sight and out of mind.

Drawers, like shelves, can be made from a variety of materials, mainly melamine, timber, plastic and wire. Choose a material to suit your storage needs and situation. Drawers have width, depth, height and varying base strength.

Roll-out shelves

Drawn and quartered

Drawers work perfectly for storage at chest height and lower. You need to be able to peer into the drawer in order to use it effectively. Shelves work best at eye level and above.

Utilise the height of drawers. This is the measurement of the clearance space between the internal base of a drawer and the bottom of the front face of the drawer above it. For top drawers, measure from the internal base of the drawer to the bottom of the fixing rail. Use these measurements to determine the maximum container height you can use in each drawer.

Measure all drawers separately, even if they look the same. The top drawer will almost always have a different height measurement than the rest of a set of drawers with identical front faces.

Divide and conquer

Drawers benefit hugely by having compartments, dividers or partitions. These create sections for contents that are prone to move about when the drawers are opened and closed. If you have some spare timber in the garage it's easy to make your own drawer dividers and you can make them to the exact specifications you need. Where would we be without our cutlery drawer dividers?

Tip

By strategically placing a few dividers into a drawer you can create several compartments.

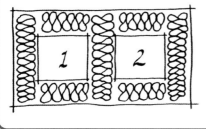
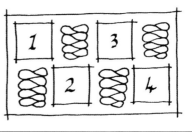

Dead end

For drawers that don't fully extend, be careful not to create dead space at the back. It's easy to have things trapped at the back. Dead space usually measures between 0 and 50 mm depending on the size of the drawer and the runners used. Always use a divider that allows access to the back of the drawer.

Droopy drawers

Overfilling drawers can cause bases to sag and drawers to stick, especially if you push the contents down while closing the drawer. You unintentionally place extra pressure on both the base and the runners.

Quick on the drawer

Drawers move in and out on runners. These runners can be fully extended or partially extended. A fully extended runner allows the drawer to roll out completely while a partially extended runner leaves a small section of the back of the drawer less accessible. It's important to know this when configuring your drawers.

Check runner strength and don't overload drawers beyond their weight capacity. Aim for fully extendable runners where possible, affordable and practical.

Double drawers have two layers of drawers within a single drawer and are particularly useful for storage of cutlery, utensils and even jewellery.

Kickboard drawers are drawers built into the kickboards of kitchens to utilise this otherwise wasted space. You can use these shallow drawers for bakeware, roasting pans, trays and platters.

One drawer with two layers of storage

Secret weapon 3: hanging rods

Whenever I go into clothing shops I just love the way everything hangs freely on hanging rods. All the hangers are the same and there is space between items. It's a pleasure to run your hand over every item on the rack. Above all, items are easy to remove and replace.

Use the same hangers within each section to create a slick look

Just hangin' around

Hanging rods come in a range of materials: chrome, wood, plastic and aluminium are the most common. Choose a material to suit your storage needs and situation.

While mostly found in wardrobes to hang dresses, shirts, skirts and trousers, hanging rods are sometimes installed in laundries to hang clothing waiting to dry, to be ironed or to be put away.

Hanging rods have length, shape and strength. Stronger, rectangular hanging rods are slowly replacing their popular, but weaker, round friends.

Aim for a length that will hold the weight of its load without sagging. You can use extra supports along the way to assist. The longer the hanging rod, the more supports you need.

Hanging rods can be attached to the side walls or to the underside of a shelf. When attached to the underside of adjustable shelves, it's really easy to move your hanging rods up and down in line with the latest hem lengths or the ages of your children. Many wardrobes are now fitted with easy-to-move hanging-rod supports, making adjustments easier. There are also easy-to-attach trapeze-like devices that allow you to hang a new rod off an existing one, giving you twice the hanging space.

Get the height right

Aim to have a range of heights for your hanging rods to suit the range of lengths of your clothing. Create sections for long, medium and short clothing. For example, you might need to accommodate long gowns, dresses, shirts, skirts and trousers. Work out your needs and fix your hanging rods accordingly. Optimise your hanging space in three simple steps.

- For each section, hang the longest item belonging to that section onto your hanging rod, complete with coathanger.
- Then move the rod up and down until you have a 50 mm to 100 mm clearance between the floor and the bottom of your garment.
- Finally, mark that spot and attach your hanging rod.

Having all your clothing hanging 50 mm to 100 mm above the floor gives you these great benefits:

- It discourages you from putting things on the floor as there is little room.
- You can vacuum and clean the floor with ease by just skimming under the clothing.
- With your hanging rods set at the lowest height for each situation you gain extra storage on the shelves above.

When using double layers of hanging rods, adjust the bottom hanging rod first and then set the higher hanging rod to the longest item, ensuring it clears the rod below by 50 mm to 100 mm.

Odd rods

Over-the-door hanging rods are convenient for hanging clothing that needs drying, airing, ironing or sorting. Hydraulic pull-down hanging rods are great for rooms with high ceilings as they allow you to hang clothing in high and often wasted space. Just use the pull-down lever to bring the rod down when required.

An over-the-door hanging rod in action

Secret weapon 4: hooks

Anyone who has a key hook knows how handy hooks can be. Whenever a hook is hung it's usually for a specific need, such as for hanging the dog's lead near the back door or for hanging the children's school bags on before and after school. Often it's the first thing that comes to mind for a quick fix for solving many of life's frequent frustrations! When I first became a mother, I installed a few removable hooks on the back of the bedroom doors to hold towels for my children. So handy! The towels don't clutter up the rest of the room, the children can reach them easily and I could easily adjust the hooks and remove them when they were no longer needed. A simple but effective 'hook' solution.

Hooks are a quick and easy way to add extra storage almost anywhere. Whether on walls, behind doors or on the sides of bookcases, a few well-placed hooks can work wonders.

Coat hooks clear clutter

Hooks include fixed or removable hooks, over-the-door hooks, hanging hooks, and fixed and free-standing coat racks.

If hooks take your fancy, here are some tips for using them:

- Ensure hooks can hold the weight of the items hanging from them. You don't want a hook and its contents falling in the middle of the night!
- S-shaped hooks can be hung from hanging rods and eliminate the need to have hooks on walls.
- Consider using a noticeboard or magnetic board with a range of hooks on it if you have a number of items to hang.
- Use hooks to hang bags, scarves and belts in wardrobes, extension cords in laundries, coats and hats in entrances, calendars on walls or kitchen doors, or jewellery on the backs of wardrobe doors.

Secret weapon 5: containers

Containers are the most popular storage solution. Just look in your plastics cupboard to see how far your obsession for containers has progressed. Many people purchase containers just for the look of them, without knowing what they will be used for. Most of these containers remain empty, cluttering up cupboards and waiting patiently to be of use. Containers love nothing more than being put to work, safeguarding the items that fill them. They happily live in drawers minding your paperclips, sit on shelves storing your sugar and hang from rods protecting your evening gown. They require minimal maintenance, they never take a holiday and they only complain when they are overstuffed!

Containers are used to hold, store or transport one or more items. They keep items clean and fresh and come in all shapes and sizes. The range includes boxes, plastic tubs, cutlery trays, jars, tins, cans and bins. The key to container use is to choose a container that is compatible with both the items stored and the storage location.

Break down the bulk

It's always better to use more containers of a smaller size than fewer containers of a larger size. The larger the container, the more it holds, the heavier it gets and the harder it is to store. If you break a large container down to two to three smaller containers you reduce the weight and the bulk and increase the storage options. The smaller containers are easier to lift, move, stack and store. Reserve the use of large containers for light items.

Load 'em up

When filling your containers with sets of rigid items—such as CDs and DVDs in your living spaces or packets of soup in your pantry—follow these five steps.

- Load contents as vertically as possible for easy visibility and access. When filling a container, it's sometimes easier to load the container while it's standing on its side.
- Place items across the shortest distance between sides, rather than along the longest distance where they will have more space to fall.
- Aim to fill any container to only 90 per cent of its capacity to allow for easy access, removal and replacement of contents.
- If the container is less than 90 per cent full, use a filler—such as scrunched-up paper—to fill the gap until you have more items to store. This stops the contents falling about and stabilises the container.
- Use dividers to break containers into sections if necessary.

Creating contented containers

Keep the following in mind and you'll find that containers are an indispensible storage item.

- If containers stack easily, they require less storage space when not in use.
- Having clear containers and lids lets you see their contents from any angle.
- Lids are optional in many circumstances, so use open containers when you can.

- Unless you are intentionally colour coding, use neutral or transparent containers.
- Aim for uniformity to create a clean look and so that you can mix and match.
- Keep in mind that round containers take up more space and are harder to arrange.
- Choose containers with castors for floor storage.
- Label your containers so you know what's in them.

Now that you have a handle on your hardware, it's time to learn some time-saving techniques that will turn your organising work into organising play! So read on.

in8 time-saving techniques

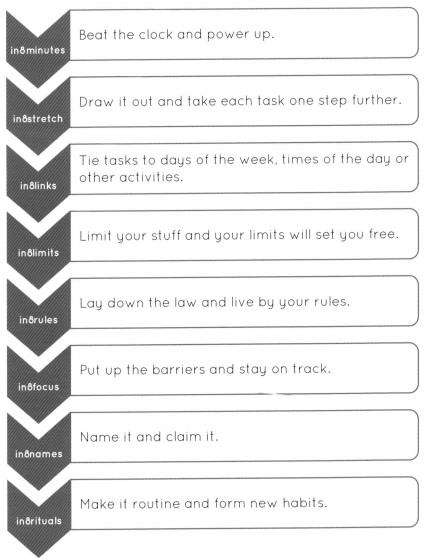

in8minutes — Beat the clock and power up.

in8stretch — Draw it out and take each task one step further.

in8links — Tie tasks to days of the week, times of the day or other activities.

in8limits — Limit your stuff and your limits will set you free.

in8rules — Lay down the law and live by your rules.

in8focus — Put up the barriers and stay on track.

in8names — Name it and claim it.

in8rituals — Make it routine and form new habits.

5

Masterclass 5: time-saving techniques

> Work expands so as to fill the time available for its completion.
>
> *C. Northcote Parkinson*

It's the little things

Sometimes little things have a big impact. The following in8time-saving techniques are little things you can do when you get bitten by the procrastination bug! We all try to put things off at times even though we know it will take us twice as long to do it later on! Later is the best friend of clutter and everything we put off is just more unfinished business cluttering up our homes and our heads.

Learn the following in8time-saving techniques and use them whenever you feel the need for that turbo boost of power!

Beat the clock: in8minutes

You know how quickly you can do something when you are under pressure. Remember the last time someone gave you short notice that they were coming to visit? You did a quick run around and achieved amazing things in a very short time. The house looked great and you enjoyed the occasion knowing all the clutter was safely parked in the laundry. With in8minutes you create the same sense of urgency by using a timer to speed up your performance. Try this: set a timer for eight minutes. Go to your bathroom and put things away, change the towels and do a general tidy up. I bet it takes *less than* eight minutes to do! It's not a spring clean but the bathroom looks very presentable. Pump yourself up with in8minute power bursts to do those mundane jobs around the house or small sections of your reorganising project. I have two favourite in8minute power bursts.

- *The in8minute email purge.* I set the timer, write down how many emails I have in my inbox and then power away. Ding, ding, ding and eight minutes later I can see just how many emails I have deleted, replied to or moved to folders. Once I see just how much can be done in8minutes, I often set the timer to go another round and after a few sessions my inbox is clear again. Such a relief!
- *The in8minute room run-around.* I set the timer for eight minutes per room in my house. I race around doing a quick straighten up and tidy, and the house is instantly fit for visitors or for the cleaners to do their thing!

Draw it out: in8stretch

This technique involves taking a task one little step further than usual. If you normally make breakfast and leave everything out while you sit down to eat, why not stretch the task to include putting away whatever you can *before* you sit down to eat? Here are two of my favourite in8stretches.

- I fold items as soon as I remove them from the clothes line or dryer, which saves on ironing time.
- I cook extra portions of casserole or soup for freezing, which saves on cooking time later on.

What in8 stretches can you put into your daily routine?

Tie them up: in8links

Have you ever gone through a week, or even a month, and realised you haven't changed the sheets or watered the plants? If you leave tasks to when you think about them, they often get neglected. in8links is a simple technique that links routine tasks to other routine tasks or memorable dates or times. If you regularly change the bed linen and do the washing on Saturday or do the ironing while watching your favourite TV show, you are already using in8links without realising it. Why not link watering the plants to rubbish collection day or washing the car to the last Sunday of the month or to when the lawns are cut? Link tasks to days of the week, times of the day or other activities such as your favourite TV show. How many tasks can you link up?

Put a lid on it: in8limits

How much is enough? The biggest issue with clutter in a disorganised home is the sheer quantity! Everyone is packed to the rafters with stuff. We are all suffering from *stuffocation*, which is a symptom of *affluenza*! A simple way to reduce what you have is to apply in8limits to every category and make a decision on how much is enough for your current lifestyle. How many pairs of shoes, handbags, shirts, trousers, wine glasses, towels, books, DVDs, TVs and radios are enough? I have placed limits on just about everything in my home and office.

- *Towels.* I have three per person in our home and two spares for guests. I now have loads of extra space in my linen cupboard.
- *Sheets.* I have two sets per bed, one on the bed and one in the wash or in the linen cupboard. This means no more stuffy, stale sheets.

It is a revelation to discover just how much you really have and liberating when you make a conscious decision on how much is enough. Your limits will set you free!

Lay down the law: in8rules

I really admire people who can say they *always* do something or they *never* do something else. For example: 'I never leave the toilet seat up', 'I always wash my hands before cooking', 'I never go to bed until the kitchen is tidy and everything is put away' or 'I never go shopping without a shopping list'. in8rules work really well for resolving your frequent frustrations and irritations. Once you identify the frustrations, create a new rule to eliminate them from your life. If you are always searching for misplaced reading glasses, allocate one spot to place them and make the rule, 'I always place my reading glasses in the bowl in the kitchen'. Most rules include *always* or *never* because that is what makes the difference between a rule and a wish. If you say, 'I will try to make my bed every morning', it's not a rule, it's just a wish! What rules can you set for yourself to overcome your frequent frustrations? What rules do you already use? Are your current rules moving you forward or holding you back?

Put up the barriers: in8focus

Do you start things and then get distracted along the way? If you do, then try some in8 focus techniques to make you more efficient and focused on the task at hand. If you have some important paperwork to do, try locking yourself in the study. This stops others interrupting you and stops you from escaping from the room! You can write your tasks on a piece of paper and stick it on the wall to remind you of what you are doing. Have a special uniform to wear while undertaking certain activities. You could wear a tracksuit for house cleaning or an apron for cooking. I have tried all these measures and they work. I regularly tie myself to my office chair until I finish what I set out to do! I always wear an apron when cooking, and my training gear when cleaning or decluttering. Make it fun, experiment and see what works for you.

Give it an alias: in8names

This technique changes your perceptions by renaming and reclaiming your space. If you call a drawer a junk drawer, guess what? Junk will live in that drawer! If you call a room a spare room, all of the spare stuff will gather there. So why not elevate the space by assigning a new and meaningful name to it? Names such as guest room, study, tea-towel drawer, library, sewing room and linen cupboard describe the space and what goes into it. I used to call the top of our stairs the landing and lots of stuff ended up landing there. I now call the space the library and have installed shelving along the walls to store all my books. The whole area has taken on a new personality and nothing just lands there anymore. For a short time it may help to use labels to remind you of what goes where, but once you get used to calling a space by its new name, the space will conform to its name. Naming also means labelling. Where necessary or appropriate, use labels to remind you of what goes where.

Make it routine: in8rituals

These are a series of activities performed in a sequence. You can set up a morning and an evening ritual, a mealtime ritual or a study ritual. It involves looking at all the activities and steps you need to undertake, estimating the time they will take and thereby creating a sort of procedure. Here is an example of a morning ritual:

- Get up and make the bed as it would be made in a five-star hotel.
- Get dressed for exercise.
- Have a cup of hot water and lemon juice and then exercise.
- Have breakfast, shower and get dressed for the day.
- Take any washing to the laundry and remove anything that does not belong in the bedroom or bathroom.

Once you get used to using a few rituals, these become habits that comfort and support you along the way. You go into autopilot mode and everything is so much easier to do.

Use the in8 time-saving techniques and use them often. Mix them up, combine them and then see what happens. Any time you get stuck, pick a technique to help get you unstuck. These techniques can be applied to any room of your home and will make getting organised much more fun.

PART II
Room by room

Congratulations on completing the masterclasses! You are now fully equipped to transform your stuffed house into a sorted home!

Each of the chapters in part II focuses on organising one room of your home.

- In **chapter 6: bathroom blitz** we will turn a cluttered bathroom into a bathing sanctuary.
- In **chapter 7: laundry hung and dried** we will finally give your laundry the respect it deserves.
- In **chapter 8: kickstart your kitchen** we will make you rethink and reassess this important room.
- In **chapter 9: bedroom boost** we will once and for all address the issue of a wardrobe full of clothes with nothing to wear.
- In **chapter 10: fresh faces for living spaces** we will give the public areas of your home a face lift.
- In **chapter 11: office overhaul** we will turn your paperwork into paperplay.
- In **chapter 12: lifting the door on garages** we will close the door on the house and complete your home makeover by going outside and turning your attention to the poor old neglected garage.

I challenge you to do a room a week. That is more than enough time for those with full-time jobs! Are you up to it? Read on and be sure to let me know!

6

Bathroom blitz

“I grew up with six brothers. That's how I learned to dance — waiting for the bathroom.”

Bob Hope

Reflections in the mirror

Anyone who has spent time waiting in line for the family bathroom knows how precious that time is when you finally gain access. You are usually in a hurry to use the toilet, to have a shower, to get ready to go out or to prepare for bed. The trouble is that someone else often wants to use the bathroom at exactly the same time. Bathrooms have peak periods where tempers are tested and patience is pushed to the limit. If it's disorganised to start with, this stampede through the bathroom leaves a battleground littered with wet towels, discarded clothing, toiletry items and worse. But this is not news to you! It's time for a bathroom blitz. Together we'll create a bathroom that is clean, organised and functional.

Because bathrooms are usually the smallest room in the house, they are a great place to begin your home organising project. Bathrooms don't take long to reorganise and they require minimal time and effort. It's great to start here if you want to practise and hone your new organising skills and see results in a short space of time.

You deserve a bathroom that shines and makes you do the same — one that meets the needs of all the family, from young ones at bath time to teenagers experimenting with the latest hair gel!

Now read on to see the **in8steps** system checklist for your bathroom blitz.

in8steps at a glance

Tick the boxes as you complete the steps for bathrooms.

Step 1: initi8 the process

☐ Identify your frequent frustrations.

☐ Set your vision and your goals.

☐ Gather your tools: set up your organising, cleaning and tool kits.

☐ Get in the mood: dress for success, turn up the music and have refreshments on hand.

Step 2: investig8 what you have

☐ Note the physical, functional and emotional elements.

☐ Draw a floor plan and take measurements as required.

☐ Discover what's in your cupboards, on shelves and in drawers. Get an overview.

☐ Note anything you need to purchase or fix.

☐ Take 'before' photos.

Step 3: consolid8 into big fat categories

☐ Set up 'Bin it', 'Gift it', 'Sell it' and 'Move it' containers.

☐ Determine your big fat categories and subcategories.

☐ Sort everything into big fat categories and subcategories.

Step 4: elimin8 what you don't use, need, want or love

☐ When in doubt about an item, ask it the critical elimination questions:
   — Do I use you? If so, how often? When was the last time? When will be the next time?
   — Do I need you? Could I borrow you or substitute you with something else?
   — Do I really want you or just the memory of you or where you came from? To preserve the memory, take a photo!
   — Do I love you? Are you of sufficient sentimental value for me to keep?

☐ Set limits for both primary and secondary storage using number, space and date as a guide.

☐ Release it! Bin the trash, gift items to charity or friends, sell items of value and move things back to their correct rooms or to secondary storage.

Step 5: alloc8 containers and locations for what you are keeping

☐ Purchase any new storage components you need. Recheck the measurements first.

☐ Allocate storage space and make any necessary adjustments.

Step 6: activ8 your space

☐ Thoroughly clean the room, including all storage surfaces and interiors.

☐ Adjust or install storage components as necessary.

☐ Place items into their new containers and locations.

☐ Label containers, shelves and drawers as appropriate.

Step 7: evalu8 how it's working

☐ Have your frequent frustrations been addressed?

☐ Have you achieved your vision and goals for this space?

☐ Does the room physically, functionally and emotionally please you?

☐ Make adjustments and finetune the system until it's running smoothly.

☐ Take 'after' photos.

Step 8: celebr8 your success and maintain the system

☐ Create a list of tasks needed for regular cleaning and maintenance.

☐ Lock your tasks into your home care schedule.

☐ Raise the bar and set new standards, new rules and rituals.

☐ Congratulations! It's time to celebrate. You did it!

☐ Collect your reward. You certainly deserve it!

Before you begin

Before you begin organising your bathroom, take any dirty clothing to the laundry, as well as any used towels, face washers, bath robes and bathmats. Remember to come straight back as this is no time to get sidetracked — the rewarding work is about to begin.

Because bathrooms are usually small, with very little bench space, you may need to place a sorting table nearby. Alternatively, you may prefer to take items from the bathroom to another room to do your sorting. Decide now what's best for you. Once that's done, grab your notebook and let's get started!

Step 1: initi8

Note your frequent frustrations. Are they the wet towels left on the floor, the overcrowded shelves and drawers, the lack of a home for your hairdryer or the pathetic-looking dish of dusty, faded, decorative soaps that welcomes visitors to the room?

Set your vision and your goals, gather your tools and get in the mood.

> ## Note it!
> It's time to list your frequent frustrations and write your vision and your goals in your notebook. If you haven't already set up your organising kit, cleaning kit and tool kit, do it now.

Step 2: investig8

Physically, your bathroom will have some, or all, of the following: bath, shower, basin, toilet, bidet, cabinets, rubbish bin, laundry hamper, toys, under-bench or wall cabinets, heating, cooling, lighting, power points, locks on doors, exhaust fans, windows and doors, as well as everything that you find in drawers, in cupboards and on benches. Some bathrooms have laundry facilities as well and many people hang clothes for drying in bathrooms and use basins for handwashing small items of clothing. Bathrooms vary in size and layout.

Functionally, bathrooms are used for dressing and undressing, bathing, grooming, toileting, reading, relaxing, romancing and perhaps washing and drying clothing. Remember that your bathroom may have to function for a variety of users: children, teenagers, adults and guests. Bathrooms also have peak periods of use, usually in the early morning and evening, which can cause congestion and necessitate schedules to manage times of use.

Emotionally, most people want their bathrooms to elicit feelings of wellbeing, warmth, cleanliness, safety, privacy and comfort.

Note it!

What physical, functional and emotional elements need to be considered in your bathroom? Take a good look around the room and note anything that needs fixing or purchasing. Take measurements if you need to, and snap a few 'before' photos before getting into the 'Do it' phase.

 # Step 3: consolid8

Sort your bathroom items into big fat categories. Lay out your sorting containers and group items together, throwing out as much as possible along the way. Here is a list of typical bathroom big fat categories with their subcategories. Use them or create your own:

- *bathing items:* soaps and body wash, shampoos and conditioners, shower caps, bubble bath and oils and children's bath toys

- *grooming items:* hair care, nail care, dental care, shaving items, beauty products, makeup and perfumes

- *toiletry items:* air fresheners, toilet paper, wipes and feminine hygiene products
- *medications:* tablets, mixtures, drops, ointments, vitamins and first-aid items
- *bathroom linen:* towels, face washers, bath mats and bathrobes
- *appliances:* electric toothbrushes, hairdryers, hair straighteners, shavers, hair clippers and electric curlers
- *cleaning products:* toilet cleaners, bathroom cleaners, cloths and sponges.

Note it!

Make a list of your big fat categories and subcategories and create new ones as you discover things along the way.

Chunk it down

Work drawer by drawer, shelf by shelf until the entire bathroom contents are in their containers. Be ruthless with anything that has just been hanging around, unused and unloved. In such limited primary space everything must earn its right to stay. The entire bathroom should take you a few hours to fully reorganise. Remember that you can do just one subcategory any time you have a spare eight minutes. Just set the timer and go, go, go!

Bella's bathroom blitz

Bella was sick of the wet towels on the floor, the open tube of toothpaste oozing its contents all over her benches and the total disarray in her cupboards and drawers. All she wanted was a nice, tidy bathroom for her family and one that her friends could use without her having to make the usual

'Excuse the mess' apology. So she set to work, tackling one category at a time. She created a container for each of her children and one for things everyone used. She threw out rusty shavers, she tipped all the half-finished shampoos into one to create her own special shampoo blend and she put all the bathroom treats received as gifts into the 'Charity' box.

Bella was quite surprised to find how little each person really needed in the bathroom. Her two daughters and her son were allocated a divided drawer each to hold their day-to-day toiletries. Each daughter also had a shelf in her bedroom wardrobe allocated to grooming. On it were makeup containers, a nail care kit, hair products and a hairdryer. The cupboard door had a mirror installed and the nearby power point was perfect for the hairdryer. The girls were delighted to be able to do their makeup in peace without everyone yelling at them to get out of the bathroom. The cupboard under the sink was stocked with toilet paper, feminine hygiene items and a supply of shampoo, conditioner and soap. A small bathroom cleaning kit for daily wipe downs and the weekly clean was placed in a caddy on the bottom shelf. A clean stock of towels was placed onto a new towel stand and a small laundry hamper was popped into a corner.

Bella looked at the stuff going into the bin and wondered how she had let it linger for so long! 'Never again!' was the promise she quietly made to herself as she locked in Saturday mornings as the weekly bathroom cleaning time.

Now that the physical and functional elements had been taken care of, Bella was off to the shops to purchase a few new decorator accessories for her bathroom to give it her personal touch.

 # Step 4: elimin8

Eliminate as much as you can by asking the following critical questions of each item you are unsure about:

- Do I use you? If so, how often? When was the last time? When will be the next time?
- Do I need you?
- Do I really want you?
- Do I love you?

Cosmetics, beauty products and fragrances go stale and old products are best disposed of. If you have switched brands, you are not going back, so let go of the old brands. Most bath salts, essences and oils languish in cupboards for years and years. Use them or lose them! Take a deep breath and out they go. Ahhh, that feels better already!

Set limits on what will be stored in primary and secondary bathroom storage space and how much you want in secondary storage space elsewhere. How many tubes of toothpaste, lipsticks, perfumes, bottles of shampoo and children's bath toys are enough? Consider the amount of storage you have and the users of the room.

 # Step 5: alloc8

Allocate containers and locations for what you are keeping. The advantage now is that you can see exactly how much stuff and space you have. The trick is to match the stuff with the space.

Organise your bathroom by allocating space by person, by function (such as hair care or nail care), or by type or shape of item (such as sprays, bottles, jars, lipsticks and perfumes). The choice is yours, and you can combine them. Do whatever makes sense to you.

Storage smarts for bathrooms

Refer to masterclass 4: getting a handle on hardware for a quick refresher, if necessary. When organising your bathing items consider the amount of storage space you have and your priorities. The bathroom is nearly all primary space so excess supplies will have to be stored elsewhere. Choose a location as near as possible to the bathroom.

Keep everything you use daily close at hand

Here are some guidelines for bathroom storage.

Splish splash!

Organise your bathing items:

* Limit the number of items in the shower to the bare necessities. Store them on shelves, in caddies or in hanging holders. Aim to have everyone use the same brand of shampoo, conditioner, soap or body wash to save having half-open bottles on the shower floor.

A shower caddy instantly declutters the shower floor

- Use liquid soaps in dispensers because these are not as messy as soaps. Use them at the basin and in the shower.
- Prevent scum and mould build-up by keeping a squeegee or cloth handy to wipe the shower dry after use.

Mirror, mirror on the wall

Organise your grooming items:

- Store creams and lotions that you use daily within easy reach.
- Set a shelf at the right height to accommodate all of your creams. They look great all in a row and you can easily identify the contents with the label facing you. If you don't have shelves, use drawers with dividers and either turn the jars on their sides or label the tops of the jars so you know what's inside.
- Your makeup kit should hold all the makeup you wear on a day-to-day basis. Have this in a portable container so it can travel with you when you are out of the house or for when you complete your makeup routine in another room because someone else needs the bathroom more urgently than you. Keep your makeup kit in the top drawer or on a handy shelf ready for action. Store extra makeup supplies in containers in a drawer or on a shelf elsewhere.
- Put together a manicure and pedicure kit with everything you need in one portable container. Now you can have a foot soak and do your nails while watching your favourite TV program, with everything you need in one container. Keep your kit on a shelf or in a drawer. Label it and it's ready to use.
- Chances are you have lots of hair products: brushes, combs, rollers, hairspray and hair treatments. So get them grouped and containerised. Items you use every day need to be in a top drawer or on a shelf within easy reach.
- Hair removal products come in various shapes and sizes, from wax strips to tubs of wax or cream to razors to electric appliances. Immediately bin old rusty razor blades and used disposable razors. Place all hair removal items into one container, label them and store them away.

- Men will need a shaving department for their shaving implements. Keep it handy in a top drawer or on a shelf.

- Put all your fragrances together: male in one group, female in another. If any are just about used up, make a point of using them first. Fragrances are often stored on counter surfaces or on open shelving where they attract dust and go stale due to heat and light exposure. It's best to keep all fragrances not used daily in their boxes in cupboards out of the light. It takes a while to go through a bottle of perfume or aftershave so it's best to replace near-empty bottles rather than to continually collect new ones that may be stored for months or years. (Apologies to those of you who have a fragrance fetish!)

- Reserve a space for guests' items if you have frequent visitors and provide occasional guests with a basket or a container for their toiletries to keep them together.

- Dental items such as dental floss, mouthwash, toothpaste and toothbrushes need to be sorted through. Throw out gunky tubes of toothpaste and old toothbrushes. Try to have one brand of toothpaste for the whole family and a small supply of toothpaste and toothbrushes in reserve. Mouthwash and dental floss can be stored on shelves or in drawers, while toothbrushes and toothpaste work best in cups on top of or below the basin, or on a shelf.

Toilet training
Organise your toiletry items:

- Always have spare toilet rolls, air freshener, a toilet brush and a lidded bin in each toilet to avoid embarrassment.

- Take toilet paper out of its packaging once it's opened. Place as many rolls as fit conveniently into an allocated space in the bathroom and toilet. Store the rest elsewhere and top up as necessary.

- Place feminine-hygiene items into containers in a drawer or into a box near the toilet.

- Install a lock on your bathroom and toilet doors to ensure privacy.

- Some people get their reading done in the bathroom. A magazine holder or box for reading material will keep the space neat.

Take your medicine
Organise your medications:

- Now is a good time to assemble a first-aid kit for the home and the car. You can put one together yourself or purchase one ready-made. Place items in a suitable container and label it clearly. Let everyone know where it is stored and you will be fully prepared for the next cut or splinter emergency!
- Keep medications in original packaging and, where necessary, add a note to clarify what it is and who it is for. Out-of-date medications should be taken back to the pharmacy for disposal. Bathrooms have high humidity so it's best not to store medications in bathrooms long-term.
- You can place each person's current medications into a separate container. General family medications for things such as coughs, colds and headaches can be placed together in another container. Keep the packaging and write additional information on the packaging and the containers if there is likely to be any confusion later on.
- If you take vitamins, keep them in a container or basket for easy access. Label your containers so you and everyone else knows what the medication is, what it is used for and who it is used by.
- You can place each container on a shelf or place all the containers into a larger one and place that on a shelf, preferably not in the bathroom. Keep it out of reach of children.

Don't throw in the towel
Organise your bathroom linen:

- Always have a fresh supply of towels and hand towels in the bathroom or nearby.
- As a rule of thumb, if you have a good washer and dryer you only need two or three towels per person and two for guests. Replace them whenever they show signs of wear.

- Give your bathroom a whole new look with a change of towel colour and new accessories. If you have two or more bathrooms, you can interchange towel colours and accessories to change the look more frequently.

- Consider having a laundry hamper in the bathroom and emptying it daily.

- How many towels you store in your bathroom is a matter of choice and space. Regardless of space, put out your best towels and start using them! You should also keep a guest set on standby. Towels are meant to envelop and caress your body, so use your nice ones. Treat yourself like a guest in your own home!

- When washing your towels, fluff them up by reducing the amount of detergent you use to about a quarter, adding a little vinegar to the final rinse cycle and allowing a few minutes in the dryer when they are nearly dry.

- If you have to stack more than five towels on top of each other, consider adding another shelf. Ideally, stack no more than two or three towels per shelf. Have folds to the front of the shelf for that designer look.

Storage smarts for families

Colour-code towels and designate a towel rail or hook for each family member.

When you have a number of people using the bathroom every morning and evening, have them do their hair, put on makeup and get dressed in their own bedrooms and leave only the essential tasks to the bathroom. A personal grooming station in each bedroom, a towel hook or rail behind the bedroom door and a bedroom laundry hamper complete the job, leaving more room and time in the bathroom for the rest of the family.

Use a basket, container or wash bag to hold personal bathroom items that can be moved between the bathroom and bedroom when needed.

> Consider rostering time in the bathroom, with each person being allotted a timeslot based on their schedule.
>
> Children's bath toys often linger in the bath long after bath time is over, trapping water and bath scum. Limit the number of toys children have in the bath. A set of stacking cups that pack away easily is sufficient to keep little ones occupied during bath time.

All curled up

Organise your appliances:

- Store appliances such as hairdryers and hair straighteners in a container in a cupboard under the basin or purchase appliance holders and attach them to walls.
- Consider installing power points inside cupboards to recharge electric shavers and toothbrushes.

A little elbow grease

Organise your cleaning products:

- Cull your cleaning supplies to a few, basic, all-purpose, non-toxic cleaners. Place your cleaning items into a caddy and store it in the bathroom or nearby.
- While bathing and showering, turn on the exhaust fan to avoid steam fogging up mirrors and raising moisture levels.
- Dry off the shower, hand basin and mirror after each use. That way your bathroom will always sparkle!

 # Step 6: activ8

Finish it all off and put everything in its place:

- Give the bathroom a thorough clean, including light fittings and exhaust fans. Your bathroom should look like the ones you admire in magazines: fresh, clean and welcoming.

- Place items in their new locations, adjusting and adding storage if necessary. Label containers.
- Decide how much you want to have out on benches. Aim for the least amount possible. Items on bathroom benches take up valuable working space.
- Lastly, add a few decorator accessories to give the room your personal touch.

 Step 7: evalu8

Well done—you've finished the 'Do it' phase! You can now stand back and admire your results and measure them against your vision and the goals you set for yourself. It's time to get your camera out to take your 'after' photos. Compare them with your 'before' photos. *Wow!* What a difference! Go back to the notes you took in the 'Plan it' phase and note your answers to the following questions.

Note it!

- Have your frequent frustrations been addressed?
- Have you achieved your vision and your goals?
- Does your bathroom physically, functionally and emotionally please you?

If you say 'no' to any of these questions, make adjustments now, or make a note to follow up within seven days. Continue to evaluate your bathroom and make changes as your lifestyle and circumstances change.

Step 8: celebr8

No bathroom is going to keep itself looking the way yours does right now. You need to add regular bathroom cleaning and maintenance to your home care schedule. So let's quickly make a list of the tasks that need to be done to keep your bathroom humming. Here is an example of timely tasks for bathrooms. Use this list or create your own.

Timely tasks for bathrooms

Daily	Weekly	Monthly	Quarterly
Dry off shower, bath and basin after use	Change towels	Clean windows	Declutter cupboards and drawers
Empty bathroom bins	Top up toilet paper, soap and so on	Clean bathroom cupboards	Clean curtains or window fittings
Use toilet brush at least once a day	Clean surfaces, mirrors and floors	Clean exhaust fans	Refresh room with new look and feel

Lock it in!

Once you have completed your own task list, add the tasks to your home care schedule. You will need to lock in times to complete each task to maintain your new-look bathroom.

Raise the bar!

It's time to set new standards, new rules and new rituals to maintain your clean, organised and functional bathroom.

Keep your 'before' and 'after' photos handy to remind yourself of how far you have come and to see the new standard you have set. Create a few new rules, such as: 'I always change the towels on Saturdays and Wednesdays', 'I always take dirty clothes to the laundry and put clean clothes away' and 'I always give the toilet a quick clean after I use it'.

String a few tasks together to create some new rituals. Your morning bathroom ritual could be something like this:

• Open window, take shower and dry off walls and shower screen.

• Put makeup on, do hair and put everything away.

• Take washing to the laundry.

Once you get into the swing of your rituals they will become habits—habits that will serve you and make life easier!

Create new rituals to guide you through children's bath times and any other stressful time periods or tasks.

Maintain it!

Now all you need to do is follow your home care schedule and live up to your new standards. It will be easy to achieve with your fresh, clean bathroom as your foundation.

Note it!

I have completed my timely tasks for bathrooms and locked times into my home care schedule.
My new rules are: _____
My new rituals are: _____

Congratulations! It's time to celebrate. You did it! You have created a bathroom that is clean, organised and functional. It's time to collect your reward for completing this room. Book in a massage, have coffee with friends, go to a show or just have a bath! You deserve it!

Are you ready for another room? Then turn to the relevant page and motor on!

7

Laundry hung and dried

> Behind every working woman is an enormous pile of unwashed laundry.

Barbara Dale

Escape the spin cycle

Is your laundry covered with so many piles of clothing that you can no longer see the floor? Can you clearly define where the dirty clothing ends and the clean clothing begins? Or does it all get mixed back together for yet another load? Is the laundry the place where you store all your spare candles, light bulbs and batteries but can't find them when they are needed in an emergency? Do you wonder what's in those shopping bags tossed in among the clothes?

It's amazing what you find in laundries. They seem to be the place where everything that doesn't have a home secretly settles until a home can be found. Many things live in the laundry for the whole of their useful lives, totally abandoned and forgotten. When we stumble across them they have long been replaced with a duplicate that is kept elsewhere. Laundry baskets seem to be the most convenient thing people grab whenever a mess needs to be scooped up and moved out of the way in a hurry. How many times have you said, 'I'll just throw it in the laundry for now'? Well, not any more. Your laundry is about to be hung and dried. Together we'll create a laundry that is clean, organised and functional.

Now read on to see the **in8steps** system checklist for your laundry makeover.

in8steps at a glance

Tick the boxes as you complete the steps for laundries.

Step 1: initi8 the process

☐ Identify your frequent frustrations.

☐ Set your vision and your goals.

☐ Gather your tools: set up your organising, cleaning and tool kits.

☐ Get in the mood: dress for success, turn up the music and have refreshments on hand.

Step 2: investig8 what you have

☐ Note the physical, functional and emotional elements.

☐ Draw a floor plan and take measurements as required.

☐ Discover what's in your cupboards, on shelves and in drawers. Get an overview.

☐ Note anything you need to purchase or fix.

☐ Take 'before' photos.

Step 3: consolid8 into big fat categories

☐ Set up 'Bin it', 'Gift it', 'Sell it' and 'Move it' containers.

☐ Determine your big fat categories and subcategories.

☐ Sort everything into big fat categories and subcategories.

Step 4: elimin8 what you don't use, need, want or love

☐ When in doubt about an item, ask it the critical elimination questions:
  — Do I use you? If so, how often? When was the last time? When will be the next time?
  — Do I need you? Could I borrow you or substitute you with something else?
  — Do I really want you or just the memory of you or where you came from? To preserve the memory, take a photo!
  — Do I love you? Are you of sufficient sentimental value for me to keep?

- ☐ Set limits for both primary and secondary storage using number, space and date as a guide.

- ☐ Release it! Bin the trash, gift items to charity or friends, sell items of value and move things back to their correct rooms or to secondary storage.

Do it Step 5: alloc8 containers and locations for what you are keeping

- ☐ Purchase any new storage components you need. Recheck the measurements first.

- ☐ Allocate storage space and make any necessary adjustments.

Do it Step 6: activ8 your space

- ☐ Thoroughly clean the room, including all storage surfaces and interiors.

- ☐ Adjust or install storage components as necessary.

- ☐ Place items into their new containers and locations.

- ☐ Label containers, shelves and drawers as appropriate.

Review it Step 7: evalu8 how it's working

- ☐ Have your frequent frustrations been addressed?

- ☐ Have you achieved your vision and your goals for this space?

- ☐ Does the room physically, functionally and emotionally please you?

- ☐ Make adjustments and finetune the system until it's running smoothly.

- ☐ Take 'after' photos.

Review it Step 8: celebr8 your success and maintain the system

- ☐ Create a list of tasks needed for regular cleaning and maintenance.

- ☐ Lock your tasks into your home care schedule.

- ☐ Raise the bar and set new standards, new rules and rituals.

- ☐ Congratulations! It's time to celebrate. You did it!

- ☐ Collect your reward. You certainly deserve it!

Before you begin

Before you begin organising your laundry, clear all surfaces, throwing out any obvious rubbish. Because laundries are usually small and cramped, you should clear all available sorting surfaces, including the tops of washing machines, dryers and benchtops. Alternatively, you may prefer to take items from the laundry to another room to do your sorting. Decide now what's best for you. I suspect your 'Move it' container is going to get a good workout here, so make it a big one! Once that's done, grab your notebook and let's get started!

 # Step 1: initi8

Note your frequent frustrations. Do they include the unwashed piles of clothes strewn across the floor, the floating items that don't belong anywhere, the wet towels on top of your new red dress or the dirty stains at the base of the washing machine? Has the lint built up to form a fine film on the walls, and when was the last time the windows were cleaned? Set your vision and your goals, gather your tools and get in the mood.

Note it!
It's time to list your frequent frustrations and write your vision and your goals in your notebook. If you haven't already set up your organising kit, cleaning kit and tool kit, do it now.

Step 2: investig8

Physically, laundries tend to be small, with minimal and often neglected storage. Your laundry will have some or all of the following: washing machine, dryer, sink, under-bench or wall cabinets, shelving, ironing board, iron, floor cleaners, exhaust fan, pet feeding stations, pet sleeping areas and laundry baskets, as well as everything that fills the cupboards and drawers.

In many homes the laundry is squeezed into a cupboard with virtually no storage or work surfaces. Access to storage is often hampered by laundry baskets, the ironing board, clothing and junk blocking the way.

Functionally, laundries are primarily used for sorting, washing, drying and ironing clothing. They are often a major thoroughfare to and from the back of the house. Pets often eat, sleep and are washed in laundries. Laundries can sometimes store sports gear and they are the refuge of last resort for items belonging elsewhere!

Emotionally, laundries are often deprived and they are usually the last room in the house to get a face lift. They also lack decorator touches. When was the last time you saw a pleasant picture or any personal touches in a laundry? As a result, laundries feel bland, uninspiring and uninviting.

Note it!

What physical, functional and emotional elements need to be considered in your laundry? Take a good look around the room and note anything that needs fixing or purchasing. Take measurements if you need to, and snap a few 'before' photos before getting into the 'Do it' phase.

Step 3: consolid8

Sort your laundry items into big fat categories. Lay out your sorting containers and group items together, throwing out as much as possible along the way. Here is a list of typical laundry big fat categories with their subcategories. Use them or create your own:

- *washing:* dirty washing, clean washing and ironing
- *laundry products:* washing powder or liquids, stain removal sprays, bleaches, softeners and ironing aid sprays
- *linen:* towels, face washers, bath mats, tea towels and tablecloths
- *cleaning equipment:* vacuum cleaners, steam cleaners, mops, buckets and brooms

- *cleaning products:* household cleaners, buckets, cleaning cloths and dusters
- *household tools:* hammers, pliers, spanners, screwdrivers, screws and nails
- *spare stuff:* candles, light bulbs and batteries
- *sewing items:* needles, pins, cottons and scissors
- *shoe-care products:* shoe polish, shoelaces, shoe brushes and cloths
- *gardening items:* hand tools and gloves
- *car-care items:* car cleaner, sponges and cloths
- *pet-care products:* feeding bowls, beds, toys, collars, leads and medications
- *gift-wrapping items:* wrapping paper, ribbons, bows, gift bags and boxes
- *vases:* small, medium and large vases.

Note it!

Make a list of your big fat categories and subcategories and create new ones as you discover things along the way.

Chunk it down

Work drawer by drawer, shelf by shelf until the entire laundry contents are in their containers. Be ruthless with anything that has just been hanging around, unused and unloved. In such limited primary storage space everything must earn its right to stay. The entire laundry should take you a few hours to fully reorganise. Remember that you can do just one subcategory any time you have a spare eight minutes. Just set the timer and go, go, go!

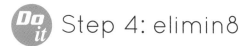

Step 4: elimin8

Eliminate as much as you can by asking the following critical questions of each item you are unsure about:

- Do I use you? If so, how often? When was the last time? When will be the next time?
- Do I need you?
- Do I really want you?
- Do I love you?

Lost in laundry limbo

In this room you will find the results of long-lost 'delayed decisions'. You may have wanted to throw something out but instead you delayed the decision by putting it into the laundry, where it has lived in laundry limbo until now. Bite the bullet and let your 'delayed decisions' go. You haven't missed them since they landed in laundry limbo!

Set limits on what will be stored in primary and secondary laundry storage space and how much you want in secondary storage space elsewhere. How many light bulbs, batteries, cleaning cloths or cleaning products are enough? Consider the amount of storage you have and the users of the room.

Step 5: alloc8

Allocate containers and locations for what you are keeping. The advantage now is that you can see exactly how much stuff and space you have. The trick is to match the stuff with the space.

Organise your laundry by allocating space by person, by function (such as 'sewing centre' or 'shoe care'), or by type or shape of item (such as sprays, bottles and boxes). The choice is yours, and you can combine them. Do whatever makes sense to you.

Storage smarts for laundries

Refer to masterclass 4: getting a handle on hardware for a quick refresher, if necessary. The laundry has a number of tasks performed in it and storage is limited, so consider what is important to you and allocate storage accordingly.

Here are some guidelines for laundry storage.

A matter of priority

One of the smallest rooms in the house is the laundry. As the name suggests, your primary focus should be on how to turn it into a streamlined, functional room where your family's clothing gets sorted, washed, dried, ironed and put away with the least possible effort and in the shortest possible time. Once that function is handled, look to what else you really want this room to do and plan around each of its functions in order of priority.

All washed up

To organise your laundry you need to allocate a space for each of three key pieces of equipment:

* *Laundry hampers.* These hold dirty clothing waiting to be washed. Ideally, they should be large enough to hold the family's wash without spilling onto the laundry floor. If you have space, use a hamper with three partitions: one

Laundry hampers in action

each for whites, coloureds and linen. This keeps the wet red towels away from your white shirts and makes it easy to see what type of washing load needs to be done next. If you have under-bench storage space, consider having your laundry hampers built into the cupboard space as three large pull-out drawers. This allows you to keep all your floor space free for moving about. If you only have room for one hamper on the floor, then make sure you have a few laundry baskets on stand-by for sorting washing into on laundry day. Extra hampers can be placed in bathrooms or bedrooms to prevent dirty clothing lining the floors of those rooms.

- *Laundry baskets.* These should all be of the same type so they stack away easily when not in use. Use them for sorting washing, for holding wet washing to be hung up or dried in the dryer, for folding into once the drying is complete and for carrying clean clothing to bedrooms. Be careful they don't stay there. The cycle ends with the clothing being put away and the washing basket being returned to the laundry, unless this basket doubles as a hamper. Hang stacked laundry baskets on hooks or place them on top of the washing machine or dryer, or on a benchtop.

- *Ironing board.* These fold flat when not in use. Find a spot against a wall or a cavity inside a cupboard in which to store it. There are purpose-specific hanging racks for ironing boards and irons and one of these may be the perfect solution for your situation. Some families have the ironing board permanently set up and this is great if space permits and if it works for you.

Done and dusted

Organise your cleaning equipment. This may include floor cleaners such as vacuum cleaners, steam cleaners, brooms and mops, as well as dusters and window cleaners. These items are meant to make cleaning easy. You need them to be stored so they can come out at a moment's notice in the event of a spill or an accident. Consolidate them by bringing them all together, including the attachments and accessories. Eliminate anything that no longer works properly or that you simply don't use any more. When you do dispose of them, get rid of all components and instructions at the same time. The key is to only keep the items that do their job well.

A can of worms

Whenever you buy a new appliance, label each of the attachments, accessories and detachable cables as soon as you unpack them. You can use sticky labels or a label maker, if you have one. This saves the frustration of trying to figure out what goes with what later on.

Label all equipment parts

Store your cleaning equipment on hanging racks or hooks or place them in a cupboard or a corner of the room. Attachments and things such as vacuum cleaner bags can be allocated a separate container and placed on a shelf or in a cupboard. Label containers and their contents as appropriate. Having an allocated place for each piece of cleaning equipment makes the task of cleaning much easier. You are more likely to continue your cleaning task if you can find the equipment easily. Otherwise it's too easy to throw your hands up and say 'I give up!'.

Floor cleaning equipment can be stored together in a corner

Hang it!

Hang extension cords by using a nifty easy-to-make cord holder. Simply take a strong piece of ribbon or string about 50 cm long and tie a knot to join the two ends. Now place the knot into the middle of an extension cord that has been wound up. Slip the other end of your holder into the loop you created when pulling through the ribbon or string and slip it through. You can now hang a bulky extension cord on a small hook.

With whitening enzymes

Organise your laundry products:

- Keep all products related to washing and ironing separate from other cleaning products.
- Place them on a shelf or in a cupboard close to the washing machine for easy access.
- Line the shelf with paper towels to protect it from spills.

Squeaky clean

Organise your house cleaning products. Gather all your house cleaning products such as detergents, disinfectants, bleaches, sprays and creams (but not your washing and ironing products, which go into your 'laundry products' big fat category). Group them all together into a big fat category called 'house cleaning products'. Don't forget all your sponges, cleaning cloths and rags.

Create a cleaning kit by allocating a cleaning bucket, container or caddy for cleaning items you use regularly. Fill it with the bare cleaning necessities. Store your cleaning kit on a shelf ready for routine or emergency cleaning jobs. Keep other special cleaners in a container to catch leaks and place it next to or behind your caddy or in secondary storage. If you only polish the silver once a year, move the silver polish out of your cleaning kit and into secondary storage. Label shelves, containers and items as necessary.

Spit and polish

Organise your shoe-care products. The 'shoe-care products' big fat category is for all your shoe polish, creams and liquids, waterproofing sprays, shoelaces, brushes and shoe dye, as well as anything else you use for shoe care. Consolidate these in a box or container. Eliminate anything that has dried out or is no longer used. Assign an appropriate shoe-kit container, basket or caddy and place regularly used items in here and spare items in another container behind or beside it. Label the container and shelf as necessary.

It's a shoe-in

Create a shoe-care pack for each shoe colour. This ensures that brushes, rags and polishes don't get mixed up. Label them clearly. Put laces into zip-lock bags so they don't get tangled. Keep excess supplies somewhere else so you don't have to rummage through all the items to polish your black shoes!

Tool up

Organise your household tools. The 'household tools' big fat category brings together hammers, screwdrivers, pliers, nails, drills, tape measures, a torch and the other items households need for fixing things such as washers for taps and picture hooks for artwork. Gather them all up into one container. Sort through them and get rid of duplicates and items that you don't use in the house. Some can go to the garage and the rest can go to others or charity. Create a one-stop tool kit with everything you need in one ready-to-go container. A tool box or a caddy works really well. Place it in a cupboard or on a shelf and label the container and shelf as preferred.

A stitch in time

Organise your sewing items. Everybody, at some time, has had to sew on a button or mend a hem. Every household needs a simple sewing kit for minor clothing repairs.

Assemble a workable sewing kit with light thread, dark thread, sewing needles, pins, a few safety pins and a good pair of scissors. Add other essential items according to your needs and place these in a portable container ready to go whenever you have a sewing emergency. Sewing boxes can also be used and there is a plethora of storage, specific to sewing, available in haberdashery stores.

If you are an avid seamstress, you will no doubt have lots of sewing items. After getting rid of any items you no longer need or use, containerise the rest. Place small containers in a larger container or place them in divided drawers. Buttons can be organised by type and placed onto safety pins to keep sets together, or placed in small containers or zip-lock bags.

Life is a tapestry

Some people store craft items in their laundry. Organise your craft items. Many people participate in crafting activities and collect lots of fiddly little bits and pieces. Bring them all together into your sorting containers for each craft. Cull all the items you no longer need and place the

A roll-out trolley holds children's craft items

rest into containers such as fishing-tackle boxes or an assortment of appropriately sized containers: try screwed-together cylindrical sets of plastic containers, jewellery organisers, ice-cube trays or even egg cartons. Use cylinders for storing knitting needles and crochet hooks. Create a craft section in a drawer, on a shelf or in a cupboard.

Crafty tip

Depending on your crafts, store each craft separately and place them in portable containers. Have duplicates of some items such as scissors and glue in each container, or place these commonly used items in their own container so they may be used with all your crafts.

Wrap it up

Organise your gift-wrapping items. Everyone has a supply of gift bags, wrapping paper, ribbons and bows. The problem is that when you go to wrap a present, the paper is wrinkled and you are confronted with a tangle of ribbons. It's time to wrap it up and get your wrapping centre in order.

Gather together all your gift-wrapping items such as wrapping paper, ribbons, bows, gift bags, adhesive tapes and scissors. Discard excess and unusable items along the way.

Tall rubbish bins or wine boxes are great for storing rolls of wrapping paper. Use wine dividers to make perfect sections for them.

Ribbons can be stored in boxes with holes for the ribbon to come through or on trouser coat hangers and hung on a hanging rod. You can also place narrow ribbon or string in jars, with a hole in the lid for the ribbon to poke through. If you recycle ribbons from gifts received from others, roll them up and place them in small zip-lock bags to avoid tangling. Have a dispenser for adhesive tape and, for that perfectly polished look, use double-sided tape, which will be hidden from view when the present is wrapped. Place tapes and scissors into a box or caddy ready for use.

Signature wrapping

Decide on using one colour or pattern for your wrapping paper and use it on every gift that you give. To individualise your gifts, be creative with how you dress them up with ribbons and bows. Your new signature look will cut down on the need to store lots of different wrapping paper.

To make a distinctive designer statement, use children's art-work to wrap gifts for family and friends.

In the right situations, newspaper or brown paper and string make perfect gift wrapping. It's all about style and how you pull it off!

Keep folded sheets of wrapping paper in a box. Get rid of wrinkled or torn paper as you won't end up using it and, if you do, you will regret it as soon as you hand the gift over!

Find a box or container where you can store gift bags vertically for easy selection and retrieval and limit these to a few of each size.

Between the sheets

Organise your linen. Linen cupboards can be located in the laundry or in other areas of the house. Regardless of where your linen is stored, it needs to be sorted. If it is in your laundry, do it now. If not, use this information later.

After gathering all your household linen together, go through each item and discard items that are worn, damaged or stained. Towels, beach towels, tea towels and sheets need to be sorted and limits need to be set.

Cull, cull, cull and then fold items so they fit the shelves to best advantage. Add additional shelving to cupboards so that you have only two to four items per stack. You will be so glad you did!

Keep sheet sets together and place each set into one of the set's pillowcases. This makes it easy to make any bed. No more hunting around—just grab the pillowcase and your whole set is there. Store sheet sets on shelves by bed size, person or room.

Keep towels folded with the fold to the front for that designer look. Fold to the depth of the shelf and limit stacks of towels to about four high to prevent them toppling over.

Get rid of torn, grungy, old tea towels. Rotate tea towels so they are always fresh. Store a supply of tea towels in the kitchen and stack the rest neatly in your linen cupboard.

Place sets of table napkins in zip-lock bags, label them and place them in a container. Wrap infrequently used tablecloths in tissue paper or place them in plastic bags. Keep regularly used tablecloths and placemats close to the table in either the kitchen or dining room, or place them on shelves in your linen cupboard.

Oops a daisy!
Organise your vases. Vases are often stored in the laundry. Where possible, keep vases in the boxes they came in. They can then be stored on their sides with the tops of the boxes facing the front for easy removal. If yours are unboxed, then simply stand them up on high shelves and create a vase department. Get rid of vases you rarely use.

Cut and polish!
Organise your car-care items. Create a car cleaning kit with all the products you use regularly. Store them in a caddy or bucket ready for use when the sun comes out and you're in a car cleaning mood. Keep it on a shelf, on a hook or in a cupboard. Secondary items go into secondary storage.

Green thumb?
Organise your gardening items. Keep all your small garden tools and secateurs in a caddy or bucket along with your gardening gloves. Store your gardening kit on a shelf, on a hook or in a cupboard. While

most gardening tools are not stored in the laundry, it can be handy to have the basics indoors.

Call in the reserves!

Organise your spare stuff. Spare light bulbs, matches, batteries and candles are often stored in laundries. Group them together, label the containers and place them in accessible areas.

Electric extension cords, double adapters and power boards can have their own department, with the cords being hung on a hook and the other items placed into an 'electricals' container.

Lights out!

Create a master list of bulb sizes for each light fitting. For example: bedroom side lamps 60w pearl, screw fitting; bedroom light 100w clear, bayonet fitting; and so on. Keep this list with your spare light bulbs and on file on your computer. This saves unnecessary ladder climbing when, to your dismay, you find you don't have a matching spare bulb!

In the dog house

Organise your pet-care products. Pet-care items are often kept in the laundry. Beds, food, accessories, feeding stations and pet medications all need storage space.

- Store food away from cleaners and chemicals to prevent chemicals leaching into the food.
- Keep walking leads handy on a hook for instant access.
- Keep flea collars and medications in clearly labelled containers and out of reach of children.
- Keep feeding bowls on drip trays to reduce mess.
- Air bedding daily and wash it regularly to avoid odour build-up.
- Have a place where items on the floor such as bedding and feeding trays can go when you need to use the room for washing, drying or ironing. If outside the door is not suitable, then place a hook on the wall or the back of the door to hang the bed on.

 # Step 6: activ8

Finish it all off and put everything in its place:

- Give the laundry a thorough clean, including light fittings and exhaust fans. Your laundry should look like the ones you admire in magazines: fresh, clean and welcoming.
- Place items in their new locations, adjusting and adding storage if necessary. Label containers.
- Decide how much you want to have out on benches. Aim for the least amount possible. Items on laundry benches take up valuable working space.
- Lastly, add a couple of decorator accessories to give the room your personal touch.

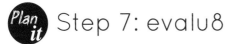 # Step 7: evalu8

Well done—you've finished the 'Do it' phase! You can now stand back and admire your results and measure them against your vision and the goals you set for yourself. It's time to get your camera out to take your 'after' photos. Compare them with your 'before' photos. *Wow!* What a difference! Go back to the notes you took in the 'Plan it' phase and note your answers to the following questions.

Note it!

- Have your frequent frustrations been addressed?
- Have you achieved your vision and your goals?
- Does your laundry physically, functionally and emotionally please you?

If you say 'no' to any of these questions, make adjustments now or make a note to follow up within seven days. Continue to evaluate your laundry and make changes as your lifestyle and circumstances change.

 Step 8: celebr8

No laundry is going to keep itself looking the way yours does right now. You need to add regular laundry cleaning and maintenance to your home care schedule. So let's quickly make a list of the tasks that need to be done to keep your laundry humming. Here is an example of timely tasks for laundries. Use this list or create your own.

Timely tasks for laundries

Daily	Weekly	Monthly	Quarterly
Place dirty washing into hampers	Wipe down appliances	Clean windows	Tidy laundry and declutter cupboards
Wash, dry and iron clothing as needed	Wash surfaces and floors	Clean laundry cupboards	Clean blinds or curtains
Clean dryer filter after each use	Empty bins	Clean exhaust vents	Refresh laundry look and feel

Lock it in!

Once you have completed your own task list, add the tasks to your home care schedule. You will need to lock in a time to complete each task to maintain your new-look laundry.

Raise the bar!

It's time to set new standards, new rules and new rituals to maintain your clean, organised and functional laundry.

Keep your 'before' and 'after' photos handy to remind yourself of how far you have come and to see the new standard you have set. Create a few new rules, such as: 'I always fold washing as soon as it comes out of the dryer or off the clothes line', 'I always put a load of washing on as soon as the basket is full' and 'I always pre-sort washing into lights, darks and household linen'.

String a few tasks together to create a few new rituals. Your 'doing the washing' ritual could be something like this:

- Select load, check pockets and wash.
- Hang out to dry.
- Fold and place into ironing basket to iron while watching the news.

You are in control! Create new rituals to guide you through linen change days and any other stressful time periods or tasks.

Maintain it!

Now all you need to do is follow your home care schedule and live up to your new standards. It will be easy to achieve with your fresh, clean laundry as your foundation.

> ## Note it!
>
> I have completed my timely tasks for laundries and locked times into my home care schedule.
>
> My new rules are: _____
> My new rituals are: _____

Congratulations! It's time to celebrate. You did it! You have created a laundry that is clean, organised and functional. It's time to collect your reward for completing this room. Book in a massage, have coffee with friends, go to a show or just have a bath! You deserve it!

Are you ready for another room? Then turn to the relevant page and motor on!

8

Kickstart your kitchen

Louis Parrish

The hub of your home

If kitchen walls could talk, what stories they could tell! This is where dreams are discussed, fights are fought, meals are made, plans are hatched and homework might be done. It's where families and friends gather to share their joys and sorrows, to discuss their aches and pains and to solve the problems of the world. Kitchens are the hub and the heart of the home.

Well, that's only half the story. Kitchen chaos reigns supreme in households around the world. Benchtops are littered with mail, cupboards are collapsing, shelves are sagging and drawers are drooping under the strain of all our stuff.

Because kitchens are the busiest and most complex room in the home, be sure to allocate enough manpower and time to the job; otherwise you may find that your family is on an enforced diet for a couple of days! You can kickstart your kitchen in stages and this is a commonsense approach. The kitchen is not the place to bite off more than you can chew! Together we'll create a kitchen that is clean, organised and functional.

Now read on to find out about the **in8steps** system checklist for kickstarting your kitchen.

in8steps at a glance

Tick the boxes as you complete the steps for kitchens.

 ## Step 1: initi8 the process

- ☐ Identify your frequent frustrations.
- ☐ Set your vision and your goals.
- ☐ Gather your tools: set up your organising, cleaning and tool kits.
- ☐ Get in the mood: dress for success, turn up the music and have refreshments on hand.

Step 2: investig8 what you have

- ☐ Note the physical, functional and emotional elements.
- ☐ Draw a floor plan and take measurements as required.
- ☐ Discover what's in your cupboards, on shelves and in drawers. Get an overview.
- ☐ Note anything you need to purchase or fix.
- ☐ Take 'before' photos.

 ## Step 3: consolid8 into big fat categories

- ☐ Set up 'Bin it', 'Gift it', 'Sell it' and 'Move it' containers.
- ☐ Determine your big fat categories and subcategories.
- ☐ Sort everything into big fat categories and subcategories.

Step 4: elimin8 what you don't use, need, want or love

- ☐ When in doubt about an item, ask it the critical elimination questions:
  - — Do I use you? If so, how often? When was the last time? When will be the next time?
  - — Do I need you? Could I borrow you or substitute you with something else?
  - — Do I really want you or just the memory of you or where you came from? To preserve the memory, take a photo!
  - — Do I love you? Are you of sufficient sentimental value for me to keep?

☐ Set limits for both primary and secondary storage using number, space and date as a guide.

☐ Release it! Bin the trash, gift items to charity or friends, sell items of value, and move things back to their correct rooms or to secondary storage.

 ## Step 5: alloc8 containers and locations for what you are keeping

☐ Purchase any new storage components you need. Recheck the measurements first.

☐ Allocate storage space and make any necessary adjustments.

 ## Step 6: activ8 your space

☐ Thoroughly clean the room, including all storage surfaces and interiors.

☐ Adjust or install storage components as necessary.

☐ Place items into their new containers and locations.

☐ Label containers, shelves and drawers as appropriate.

Step 7: evalu8 how it's working

☐ Have your frequent frustrations been addressed?

☐ Have you achieved your vision and your goals for this space?

☐ Does the room physically, functionally and emotionally please you?

☐ Make adjustments and finetune the system until it's running smoothly.

☐ Take 'after' photos.

Step 8: celebr8 your success and maintain the system

☐ Create a list of tasks needed for regular cleaning and maintenance.

☐ Lock your tasks into your home care schedule.

☐ Raise the bar and set new standards, new rules and rituals.

☐ Congratulations! It's time to celebrate. You did it!

☐ Collect your reward. You certainly deserve it!

Before you begin

Before you kickstart your kitchen, clear the decks. Wash and dry the dishes and clean the sink. Clear all the benchtops, disposing of anything not needed and putting other items back where they belong. Sweep the floor and empty the kitchen tidy. For extra sorting surfaces make space in an adjoining room, preferably one with a table and other potential sorting surfaces. If you have a portable table, it's time to put it to work. Once that's done, grab your notebook and let's get started!

 # Step 1: initi8

Note your frequent frustrations. What annoys you most about your kitchen? Does it take twice as long as necessary to find anything you need? Do you have to move five things in order to get one out? Can you see your kitchen benches or are they hiding under an avalanche of stuff? Have you run out of milk for the third time this week? I'm sure the list will be long and that's fantastic because by the time you have completed your kitchen kickstart your frustrations will be a thing of the past.

When it comes to setting your vision, your goals and a budget for your kitchen, it's important to remember that you and your family spend a lot of time in this room and you need to take into account its many users and its many functions. So be prepared to allocate a reasonable amount of time and money to this room. Unless you have a whole day or two to set aside, it's best to organise your kitchen one category at a time, eliminating what you don't need and rearranging it into its new location section by section.

Set your vision and your goals, gather your tools and get in the mood.

Note it!

It's time to list your frequent frustrations and write your vision and your goals in your notebook. If you haven't already set up your organising kit, cleaning kit and tool kit, do it now.

 Step 2: investig8

Physically, kitchens have benchtops, storage cupboards, pantries, hotplates, ovens, microwaves, refrigerators, freezers, dishwashers, sinks and a whole host of crockery, cutlery, cookware, electrical appliances, glassware and foodstuffs. Kitchens also have lighting, windows, power points, plumbing and layout, which all need to be considered when rearranging your storage solutions. The age and condition of the kitchen is also a major physical factor.

Functionally, a kitchen is the hub of the home. It is the family meeting, eating and greeting place. It's where meals are prepared, cooked, served and eaten. There's a lot of chopping, mixing, whipping, slicing, peeling, dicing, frying, boiling, grilling, baking, eating, drinking and washing up going on. Students sometimes do their homework there, little ones play underfoot, and adults read newspapers and pay the bills in the kitchen. There are many functions performed in the kitchen and it's good to note them and take them all into consideration. Be sure to consider every person in your household and any of their special needs.

Emotionally, kitchens are the heart of the home. The aroma of freshly made coffee, bread or cakes draws in family members from all over the house. It's where people chat about their day, discuss issues over a cup of tea and recharge their emotional batteries. Think about how you feel in your kitchen now and how you would like to feel.

Note it!

What physical, functional and emotional elements need to be considered in the kitchen? Take a good look around the room and note anything that needs fixing or purchasing. Take measurements if you need to, and snap a few photos before getting into the 'Do it' phase.

 Step 3: consolid8

Sort your kitchen items into big fat categories. Lay out your sorting containers and group items together, throwing out as much as possible along the way.

Because of the sheer number of items in this room, it's best to work through one big fat category at a time, consolidating, eliminating, allocating and activating space before going on to the next big fat category. So please read through all the 'Do it' steps before proceeding.

The order in which you tackle your categories will be determined by what you pull out and where it needs to go next. For example, you may take your pots and pans out of one cupboard but decide to place them in a new location. You would have to clear out the new location to make room for the pots and pans, and the stuff you cleared out would become your next category or categories. Here is a list of typical kitchen big fat categories with their subcategories. Use them or create your own:

- *cookware:* pots, saucepans and frying pans
- *bakeware:* baking trays, casserole dishes, ovenware, cake tins, muffin pans, roasting pans and dishes, and cooling racks
- *cutlery:* knives, forks and spoons
- *utensils and gadgets:* tongs, potato peelers, wooden spoons, ladles, egg flippers, measuring spoons, skewers, strawberry hullers, zesters, graters, bean stingers and spatulas
- *crockery:* dinnerware, plates, bowls, cups and saucers
- *children's plastic dinnerware:* cups, mugs and plates
- *drinkware:* glasses, cups and mugs
- *serving and preparation:* serving platters and trays, chopping boards
- *linen:* tea towels, placemats, tablecloths and napkins
- *plasticware:* containers, lids, mixing bowls, salad spinners and salad bowls
- *wraps:* cling wrap, tin foil, freezer bags, baking paper and rubbish liner bags

- *electrical appliances:* mixers, microwave ovens, deep fryers, rice cookers, blenders, toasters and kettles
- *cleaning products:* dishwashing powder or liquid, sponges, sprays and disinfectants
- *pantry:* cereals, crackers and biscuits, cans, bottles, pasta, spices and so on
- *refrigerated items:* all items in the refrigerator and freezer
- *medications:* first aid, tablets and vitamins (see also chapter 6: bathroom blitz)
- *paperwork:* in-tray, reading material such as newspapers and magazines, bills, notices and mail (see also chapter 11: office overhaul).

Note it!

Make a list of your big fat categories and subcategories and create new ones as you discover things along the way.

Chunk it down

Work drawer by drawer, shelf by shelf until the entire kitchen contents have been through the 'Do it' phase. Be ruthless with anything that has just been hanging around, unused and unloved. The entire kitchen should take you a day or two to fully reorganise. Remember that you can do the kitchen in stages or do just one small area any time you have a spare eight minutes. Just set the timer and go, go, go!

Kate's kitchen

Kate had a love–hate relationship with her kitchen. Her inner chef was longing to create healthy meals for her family and to entertain and delight her friends. While she had every gadget, appliance and cookbook imaginable, the family fed on fast food and caved in to convenience meals. The kitchen was a permanent mess and opening cupboards was always a mystery experience. Kate never knew what lurked within; although she could be sure it was not what she was looking for! Kate was sick of her chaotic kitchen and wanted to stop wasting her time, money and energy but didn't know where to start. She thought she had to do the whole kitchen at once and the prospect daunted her so much that she just kept putting it off. The **in8steps** system enabled her to organise her kitchen section by section without creating a major disruption to her busy life. By investing about an hour a day, Kate totally transformed her kitchen within two weeks. Each day set a new standard for the next and, buoyed by a series of small successes, she was motivated and inspired to continue until the job was done.

Her goal was to have a kitchen that her family loved being in and one in which it was easy to prepare healthy meals at a moment's notice. She wanted to be able to go to a cupboard confident that she could find what she wanted within a few seconds. She never again wanted to be confronted with stacks of platters waiting to topple at the slightest movement.

 Step 4: elimin8

Eliminate as much as you can by asking the following critical questions of each item you are unsure about:

- Do I use you? If so, how often? When was the last time? When will be the next time?
- Do I need you?
- Do I really want you?
- Do I love you?

- Are you out of date? Check the 'use-by' dates on all perishables.

Set limits on what will be stored in primary and secondary kitchen storage space and how much you want in secondary storage space elsewhere. How many wine glasses, mugs, plastic takeaway containers, potato peelers or tea towels is enough? Consider the amount of storage you have and the users of the room.

 Step 5: alloc8

Allocate containers and locations for what you are keeping. The advantage now is that you can see exactly how much stuff and space you have. The trick is to match the stuff with the space.

Organise your kitchen by allocating space by person (for example, children's dinnerware or snacks), by function (for example, baking, cooking, serving, washing up and paperwork), or by type or shape of item (for example, cans, cereals, dry goods, pasta, stemmed glassware, salad bowls, tumblers and egg cups). The choice is yours, and you can combine them. Do whatever makes sense to you.

Note it!

How are you going to allocate the space in your kitchen? Do you prefer to organise by person, by function, by type or shape of item, or by a combination of these? Consider everybody's needs, look at what you are working with and make a decision. Measure the space and decide on containers that best suit.

Go figure!

As everyone's kitchen is unique in its configuration, I will take you through some kitchen basics that will help you decide what goes where. The kitchen is like a big jigsaw puzzle and each part is critical to the finished product. Be prepared to do a bit of swapping and changing to find the right fit for you. The more you can do in your head or on paper, the less you need to do physically.

Who's down there?

Under-bench storage usually comes in five forms and you may have a combination of them:

- shelves behind cupboard doors
- roll-out drawers behind cupboard doors
- drawers
- corner cupboards
- dead corners.

We'll go through each of them so you fully understand their advantages, their limitations and their potential before you get all excited and pull everything out of your kitchen without a plan of attack.

Peek a boo!

Shelves behind cupboard doors are the most common form of under-bench storage because they are the cheapest to construct. If you have these, as a general rule you should invest in roll-out drawers if you can. If not, then you should at least consider additional shelves in the cupboards to provide extra storage. If you have fixed shelves these may need to stay, but you can add extra shelves in between the fixed ones. I've never met a cupboard that didn't benefit from an extra shelf or two.

If you are stuck with under-bench shelves you can create a drawer effect by using containers. Simply use containers or sturdy trays to fit the depth of the shelf. Fill these with items you need to store and pull them forwards or completely out to access the contents. Adjust the shelf to suit the height of the 'drawer' containers. Label the front of the containers or the shelves to put the icing on the cake.

On track

If you have roll-out drawers behind cupboard doors you are well on your way to being organised. The best way to optimise space is to have the roll-out drawers filled with items that use the height of the drawer. They are especially good for storing heavy crockery, cups and mugs and can also be used for pots and pans.

Pots in a roll-out drawer

Don't push me!

Drawers are the ideal under-bench storage, provided you fill them with the most suitable items. You really have to work with and utilise the height or clearance of the drawer to its best possible advantage. Most homes have at least one set of drawers in which cutlery, utensils, kitchen linen and wraps are stored. If you are fortunate enough to have drawers in all your under-bench storage you are already at a great advantage. You can maximise your drawer storage by rearranging what you store and how you store it.

Just the right angle

Corner cupboards are always a bit tricky. The first thing to do is check how many shelves you have in your corner cupboard and see if they are adjustable or fixed. Most corner cupboards come with only one shelf. If it is fixed you cannot move the shelf so you need to get a bit creative. Read on to see if the following solutions will suit your situation.

Corner cupboards have deep recesses that are really difficult to access. A clever way to deal with them is to use a number of identical containers of a depth and height slightly smaller than the depth and height of the shelves in the corner cupboard. Place the containers along one back wall of the cupboard so that the container closest to the door opening slides out easily and freely. Then place another container or two against the other back wall, with at least one of them able to slide forwards freely through the other door opening. Now to access anything in the cupboard you only need to move a container or two. Store infrequently used items such as Christmas tableware and plastic containers, plastic tableware or baking pans in the containers closest to the door.

There are also purpose-built solutions, such as lazy Susans **Corner cupboards in action** and 'magic corners', where hardware and fittings are attached to the doors to bring the contents of the corner out to greet you.

Corner cupboards can also work brilliantly for pots and pans. Place pots and pans, complete with lids, onto shelves with handles facing forward. Add a shallow shelf at the top to fit your frying pans.

Corner cupboards usually have one fixed or adjustable shelf in the middle of the cavity. As a general rule, it is almost impossible to fit a complete corner shelf into a corner cupboard without removing the benchtop. So, to get additional storage into your corners you can add shelves using step shelves or by drilling holes and attaching shelves to the back and side walls one side at a time.

Your corner cupboards are now fully functional without any dead space. Enough storage for a gourmet chef!

Call the undertaker

Dead corner cupboards are those located in corners that do not have a full corner cupboard door. The door that yo1u do have only accesses the space immediately behind it and the inaccessible corner is considered dead because the items stored there are very difficult to reach. The simplest solution is to use a number of identical containers with one or two going into the dead corner. One container should slide out freely. To remove the dead corner containers, remove the freely sliding container and slide the dead corner containers sideways and then out.

Look up now!

Cupboards above benches usually don't benefit from drawers as they are too high to peer into. As a general rule drawers cease to be functional at about chest height. However, having containers on these shelves can be hugely beneficial in bringing the contents down to the bench rather than having to search on the shelf for the item you want. Of course, you can only use containers for lightweight items if they are to be stored on the higher shelves.

A fabulous way to use the higher shelving above benches is for platters. Place a platter rack onto the top shelf and load your platters onto the rack. You can now easily remove any platter you want in a single move. This usually requires a full-depth above-bench cupboard.

It's cool

Many cabinet makers install cupboards over the refrigerator. They are usually not the full depth of the refrigerator, to allow for ventilation. These cupboards are often used for cookbooks, which is a good use of this space, if you can reach the books and see the titles easily.

Up high but within easy reach!

If not, consider installing four shelves into the cupboard with about eight and a half centimetres between them. Store your bakeware and some platters on these shallow shelves. I have done this and it is my favourite kitchen storage solution. Everyone I show is equally impressed.

Mind the S-bend!

The cupboards under sinks often contain lots of pipes and some electrics servicing the sink, dishwasher and water filter. This limits your under-sink storage options. Depending on your circumstances, you may be able to install a roll-out drawer or use containers that fit between the plumbing to hold cleaning equipment or other items.

An under-sink slide-out basket brings everything to you

A spark park

If you have an appliance centre, try to ensure the heaviest appliances are stored at waist height. Store your lightweight electrical appliances on higher shelves and place them in containers if that makes them easier to bring down.

If you need to install power points into the cupboard, make sure they are above the appliance for easy access and for maximum use of the depth of the cupboard. There is no point having a power supply right behind the microwave oven if it becomes inaccessible once the microwave oven is placed into the cupboard

All appliances in one place ready for action

or if the additional room for the power point and the plug causes the microwave oven to be too deep for the cupboard. I speak from personal experience here!

If your appliances have lots of attachments, create attachment containers and place these on shelves higher up in your appliance centre for easy access. Bind any cords neatly, label the containers and you are ready for action.

Storage smarts for kitchens

Refer to masterclass 4: getting a handle on hardware for a quick refresher, if necessary. When organising your kitchen items consider the amount of storage space you have and your priorities. You and your family use this room every day, so make it a place they enjoy using and being in. Look for every opportunity to convert secondary storage into primary storage to make everything as accessible as possible.

Here are some guidelines for efficient kitchen storage.

Don't stir the pot

Organise your cookware:

- Store pots and pans in corner cupboards, in drawers or on shelves in a single layer with their lids on.
- Stack pots on shelves or in drawers and store lids in lid holders on the backs of doors or place them in a container near the pots and pans if you have limited storage.

Preheat to 90 degrees

Organise your bakeware:

- Baking trays should be stored vertically in narrow cavities or vertically in containers and placed on a high shelf.
- Cake tins and cooling racks should be stored vertically by shape. Interlock sets together to maximise space. Place them in containers and store them in corner, deep or dead cupboards.
- Because a container filled with tinware is lightweight, consider placing a container full of cake tins on high shelving. They are out of the way until baking day and, being lightweight, are easy to get down.

- Baking and roasting dishes store well on shallow shelving so you can remove one item at a time as needed. An ideal spot is above the fridge, but you can add shelves in any cupboard. Add four narrowly spaced shelves (about eight and a half centimetres apart) and you will never again struggle with stacked baking dishes!

Take the right fork

Organise your cutlery:

- Most cutlery drawers already have dividers in them, but are they the best dividers for your needs? If not, now is the time to replace them with ones that have the sections you need.

Double up your cutlery storage

- Use cutlery dividers that are deeper rather than shallower. You can purchase deeper containers from specialist container stores or restaurant suppliers.

- If you have more than one set of cutlery to store, consider turning your single drawer into a double drawer.

Peel those spuds

When organising your utensils:

- Everyday utensils can easily be stored in a container on a benchtop.

- They can be hung from a rack or holder on a wall.

- Most people store utensils in drawers, so optimise your storage by using containers or dividers to create sections.

Use dividers to stop utensils slipping about

Is the table set?

When organising your crockery:

- Mealtimes are busy, so your crockery needs to be easy to access in one simple movement.

- Each type of dish needs its own stack: dinner plates with dinner plates, bowls with bowls (not dinner plates with bowls stacked on top).

- Add extra shelves to reduce stack sizes.

- Crockery stores well in drawers and roll-out drawers, but always check the drawer's weight capacity. Crockery is heavy and the drawers need to have a strong base and heavy-duty runners.

Crockery storage to die for

Bottoms up!

When organising your drinkware:

- Tumblers, water glasses and stemmed glasses store well on shelves in soldier rows, one behind the other.

- All types of glasses may benefit from the 'top and tail' technique if their rim is larger than their base. Place one glass on its base, followed by one on its rim. Repeat until all glasses are in a row.

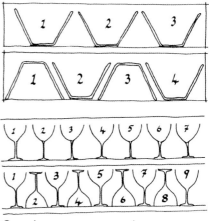

Create more space by topping and tailing your drinkware

- Store glasses in drawers fitted with non-slip drawer liners or on over-bench shelving.
- Store glasses on shelves according to their height: shortest glasses at the bottom with tallest glasses on top shelves.
- Cups are short and mugs are taller, so adjust shelves and give them a shelf each where possible. Mugs may also benefit from the 'top and tail' technique.
- Cups and mugs store well in drawers. Add the milk jug and sugar bowl and you will always be ready for a cup of tea or coffee!

Are you being served?

When organising your servingware:

- Platters love to stand proud in platter racks or holders —no more jumbling around to get the platter of your choice. Store them just above head height where they will be easy to reach, remove and replace.

Your platters love living the high life

- Platters also work well on a series of shallow shelving each holding a single layer of platters. Space shelves about eight and a half centimetres apart and layer away.
- Serving trays can be stored with chopping boards on their sides in a narrow cupboard. Against the side of a cupboard also works well, but place a container on the other side to keep them stable.
- Serving trays can also be stored with platters if size is compatible.
- Salad bowls can be stored in drawers or on shelves in single layers or stacked by size and shape. Consider using the 'top and tail' technique to efficiently stack your bowls.

See-through solutions
Organise your plastic storage containers:

- Plastics are made to store things in. Don't waste valuable storage space storing lots of empty plastic containers. Put them to work!
- Have a small selection of plastic containers on standby and store them in containers in high spaces or in corner cupboards.
- If possible, choose clear containers with clear lids so you can see the contents.
- Stack containers of the same size together to minimise the storage space you use and to keep them neat and tidy.
- Reduce the need for plastic containers for the freezer. Try this:
  - Place a plastic bag into a container.
  - Place food for freezing into the plastic bag and place this in the freezer.
  - Once frozen, remove the bag from the container, double wrap it and label it.
  - Now the container is ready for work again and all your frozen food will be the same shape and easy to stack and store!

Dining in the doll's house
Organise your children's plastic dinnerware:

- Small children usually have a supply of plastic cups, mugs, bowls, plates and cutlery that can slip and slide all over the place. Store these in low drawers with dividers to keep the contents in check.
- Consider having one container filled with plastic dinnerware on a low shelf or in a roll-out container on the floor of a walk-in pantry. Whenever the children need an item, they have an easy-to-reach, one-stop spot where they can get what they need.

I've been foiled

Organise your wraps:

- Wraps such as cling wrap, tin foil, baking paper and paper towels store well in dispensers or drawers. Keep one of each kind in primary storage and spares in secondary storage.
- Rubbish-bag liners and freezer bags can be stored with wraps, or in a container under the sink, or on a shelf.
- Plastic bags awaiting re-use can be pushed into long, tube-shaped bags and hung from a hook or placed in a drawer.

I'll wash, you dry!

Organise your kitchen linen:

- Tea towels can be placed on shelves or in drawers.
- Store eight to ten tea towels in the kitchen and the rest in your linen storage area and top them up as needed. Your kitchen drawer should not be overfilled.
- Add to this drawer anything else that is linen-related such as oven mitts, an apron and maybe some face washers and bibs if you have young children.
- Use hooks behind doors, oven handles or hanging rods to hang tea towels and aprons, and change them each night.
- Tea towels get grubby quickly so consider buying dark colours.
- Store placemats on a shallow shelf or in a drawer close to the table.
- Store serviettes and napkins in a drawer close to the table or with placemats.

Plug it in!

Organise your electrical appliances:

- Place electrical appliances on shelves or in drawers according to height, weight and usage.
- Some items, such as the kettle or toaster, usually stay out on the kitchen bench.

Destroy the appliance alliance

Let's own up: we've all bought a useless fad appliance at one time or another, right? Corn poppers, waffle irons, breadmakers... the list goes on. Now we are paying the price in terms of storage space.

What do you really use? What will you never use again? Make some decisions about what needs to be stored in primary and secondary storage space and what needs to leave the house. Ensure that items you use all the time are readily accessible and near power sources. Store heavy appliances at waist height and below. Lighter appliances can be stored higher up. Containerise all the bits that go with appliances and label the containers. Use ties or rubber bands on cords to stop the tangle.

Spick and span

Organise your cleaning products:

- Place cleaning products into containers or caddies that fit underneath the sink.

- Use backs of cupboard doors to install storage baskets if space is tight.

- Limit your storage of kitchen cleaning products to the ones you use every day in the kitchen. Keep other cleaning products in the laundry.

- Use a detergent dispenser at the sink and keep all other items out of sight until ready for use.

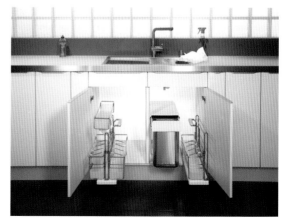

The perfect under-sink solution

- Childproof the product cleaning cupboard, or area, if you have small children.

Don't talk rubbish!

Organise your kitchen waste:

- Use a separated bin system to store rubbish, recycling and compost waste.

- Have bins in sizes to match your family size. You don't want rubbish hanging about for too long and you don't want to be emptying the bins every few hours.

- If you can, install bins in cupboards just under the kitchen bench. That way they are easy to access while preparing food and cleaning up after meals.

A compact, sealed rubbish bin with bonus vegetable storage

Food for thought

Organise your pantry:

- Date-check all pantry items and place anything approaching its use-by date into one container. Plan your meals around these foods first and then around the other items you have in the pantry to keep the stock rotating.

- Canned foods and jars should be stored on eye-level shelving in soldier rows.

- Staples and dry goods should be decanted into see-through containers that hold at least one kilogram of flour, sugar or rice. Place them in containers on shelves or in drawers. Label both the container and the lid to avoid mixing up foods that look similar (for example, flours).

Pantry storage with secondary storage on the top shelf, roll-out spice shelves and containerised pantry items

- Spices may be stored by type (sweet, savoury, Italian, Indian), by name or by dish. Store them on shallow shelving or in shallow drawers or spice racks.

- Bottles should be at waist level or below and stored by height. They can be placed on a shelf in narrow, long containers that can be pulled out like drawers when needed. You can also purchase special-purpose door hardware to hold bottles on the backs of doors or to roll them out on from inside cupboards.

- Packaged foods should be kept in original packaging, placed into containers and put on shelves. Keep like with like. Soups, snacks, pasta and baking items are natural categories.

- Potatoes and onions need ventilation. Keep them in open containers with paper towels on the bottom to absorb moisture and to catch any dirt and onion skins.

Spice it up!

The big chill

Organise your refrigerator:

- Date-check all refrigerator items and place anything approaching its use-by date into one container. Plan your meals around these foods first and then around the other items you have in the refrigerator to keep the stock rotating.

- Use containers for dairy foods, condiments and leftovers. If you eat lots of fruits and vegetables, purchase an extra couple of crispers to store them in and keep them fresh.

> ## Tip
>
> Once you have opened refrigerated items, write the date on the item so that you know the age of the contents, especially if they are in long-life containers. Long-life milk, cheeses, cream and jars of condiments all benefit from a permanent marker date on the lid or on the bottom to indicate their age since opening. So now when something says, 'Refrigerate after opening and consume within seven days', you will be in control and won't be doing the salmonella waltz!

The iceworks

Organise your freezer:

- Date-check all freezer items and place anything approaching its use-by date into one container. Plan your meals around these foods first and then around the other items you have in the freezer to keep the stock rotating. Create a master list of what you have.

Keep like with like in the freezer

- Purchase containers to fit your freezer and stack single portions of chicken in one, beef in another, mince in another and frozen vegetables in another. Keep sufficient supplies for a couple of weeks only and rotate items after shopping by placing the freshest item under the existing frozen ones.

- Label everything in the freezer with name and date.

 # Step 6: activ8

Finish it all off and put everything in its place:

- Give the kitchen a thorough clean, including light fittings and exhaust fans. Your kitchen should look like the ones you admire in magazines: fresh, clean and welcoming.

- Place items in their new locations, adjusting and adding storage if necessary. Label containers.

- Decide how much you want to have out on benches. Aim for the least amount possible. Items on kitchen benches take up valuable working space.

- Last, add a few decorator accessories to give the room your personal touch.

Step 7: evalu8

Well done—you've finished the 'Do it' phase! You can now stand back and admire your results and measure them against your vision and the goals you set for yourself. It's time to get your camera out to take your 'after' photos. Compare them with your 'before' photos. *Wow!* What a difference! Go back to the notes you took in the 'Plan it' phase and note your answers to the following questions.

Note it!

- Have your frequent frustrations been addressed?

- Have you achieved your vision and your goals?

- Does your kitchen physically, functionally and emotionally please you?

If you say 'no' to any of these questions, make adjustments now or make a note to follow up within seven days. Continue to evaluate your kitchen and make changes as your lifestyle and circumstances change.

 # Step 8: celebr8

No kitchen is going to keep itself looking the way yours does right now. You need to add regular kitchen cleaning and maintenance to your home care schedule. So let's quickly make a list of the tasks that need to be done to keep your kitchen humming. Here is an example of timely tasks for kitchens. Use this list or create your own.

Timely tasks for kitchens

Daily	Weekly	Monthly	Quarterly
Wash, dry and put dishes away	Wipe down appliances	Clean refrigerator	Tidy pantry and declutter cupboards
Empty kitchen bins	Clean hotplates and oven	Clean windows	Clean blinds or curtains
Sweep floor	Check refrigerator contents	Replace sponges	Wipe down walls
Clean sink and benches	Wash floors	Clean kitchen cupboards	Refresh room with new look and feel
Change tea towels and dish cloths	Top up dispensers in dishwasher and on sink	Clean exhaust filters	
Wipe hotplates and oven after use	Plan meals and create shopping list		

Lock it in!

Once you have completed your own task list, add the tasks to your home care schedule. You will need to lock in a time to complete each task to maintain your new-look kitchen.

Raise the bar!

It's time to set new standards, new rules and new rituals to maintain your clean, organised and functional kitchen.

Keep your 'before' and 'after' photos handy to remind yourself of how far you have come and to see the new standard you have set. Create a few new rules such as: 'I never leave dirty dishes in the sink', 'I always clean my refrigerator out the day before rubbish day' and 'I do an in8minute tidy-up every evening before bedtime'.

String a few tasks together to create some new rituals. Your bedtime kitchen ritual could be something like this:

- Set the timer and, in8minutes or less, put everything away in the kitchen.
- Empty the dishwasher, change tea towels and dishcloths, wipe down the sink and empty the bins.

I bet you will have time to spare!

Create new rituals to guide you through mealtimes and any other stressful time periods or tasks.

Maintain it!

Now all you need to do is follow your home care schedule and live up to your new standards. It will be easy to achieve with your fresh, clean kitchen as your foundation.

> ## Note it!
>
> I have completed my timely tasks for kitchens and locked times into my home care schedule.
> My new rules are: _____
> My new rituals are: _____

Congratulations! It's time to celebrate. You did it! You have created a kitchen that is clean, organised and functional. It's time to collect your reward for completing this room. Book in a massage, have coffee with friends, go to a show or just have a bath! You deserve it!

Are you ready for another room? Then turn to the relevant page and motor on!

9

Bedroom boost

> Women usually love what they buy, yet hate two-thirds of what is in their closets.

Mignon McLauchlin

Bedroom boost and wardrobe workout

There is nothing more soothing than walking into your bedroom to find the bed made as in a five-star hotel, the room looking clean and tidy, a framed photo of the family by the bedside lamp and an organised wardrobe full of clothes you love to wear. If you think this is just a dream, you are not alone. The reality is that horizontal wardrobes, better known as 'floordrobes', are rapidly replacing vertical ones! Clothing is draped over furniture, strewn across floors and piled into corners. Bedrooms across the country are littered with old reading material, dirty tissues and half-empty coffee cups. It's time to wake up from this nightmare!

Your bedroom is the first thing you see every morning and the last thing you see every night. It's the one room in the home where you can really express your personality and that you can call your own. Bedrooms are fun to organise because you get reacquainted with your wardrobe, discovering long-forgotten treasures and quite a few fashion disasters along the way. Together we'll create a bedroom that is clean, organised and functional!

Now read on and I'll reveal the **in8steps** system checklist for your bedroom boost and wardrobe workout.

in8steps at a glance

Tick the boxes as you complete the steps for bedrooms.

 ## Step 1: initi8 the process

☐ Identify your frequent frustrations.

☐ Set your vision and your goals.

☐ Gather your tools: set up your organising, cleaning and tool kits.

☐ Get in the mood: dress for success, turn up the music and have refreshments on hand.

 ## Step 2: investig8 what you have

☐ Note the physical, functional and emotional elements.

☐ Draw a floor plan and take measurements as required.

☐ Discover what's in your cupboards, on shelves and in drawers. Get an overview.

☐ Note anything you need to purchase or fix.

☐ Take 'before' photos.

 ## Step 3: consolid8 into big fat categories

☐ Set up 'Bin it', 'Gift it', 'Sell it' and 'Move it' containers.

☐ Determine your big fat categories and subcategories.

☐ Sort everything into big fat categories and subcategories.

 ## Step 4: elimin8 what you don't use, need, want or love

☐ When in doubt about an item, ask it the critical elimination questions:
   — Do I use you? If so, how often? When was the last time? When will be the next time?
   — Do I need you? Could I borrow you or substitute you with something else?
   — Do I really want you or just the memory of you or where you came from? To preserve the memory, take a photo!
   — Do I love you? Are you of sufficient sentimental value for me to keep?

☐ Set limits for both primary and secondary storage using number, space and date as a guide.

☐ Release it! Bin the trash, gift items to charity or friends, sell items of value and move things back to their correct rooms or to secondary storage.

Step 5: alloc8 containers and locations for what you are keeping

☐ Purchase any new storage components you need. Recheck measurements first.

☐ Allocate storage space and make any necessary adjustments.

Step 6: activ8 your space

☐ Thoroughly clean the room, including all storage surfaces and interiors.

☐ Adjust or install storage components as necessary.

☐ Place items into their new containers and locations.

☐ Label containers, shelves and drawers as appropriate.

Step 7: evalu8 how it's working

☐ Have your frequent frustrations been addressed?

☐ Have you achieved your vision and your goals for this space?

☐ Does the room physically, functionally and emotionally please you?

☐ Make adjustments and finetune the system until it's running smoothly.

☐ Take 'after' photos.

Step 8: celebr8 your success and maintain the system

☐ Create a list of tasks needed for regular cleaning and maintenance.

☐ Lock your tasks into your home care schedule.

☐ Raise the bar and set new standards, new rules and rituals.

☐ Congratulations! It's time to celebrate. You did it!

☐ Collect your reward. You certainly deserve it!

Before you begin

Before you start organising a bedroom, make the bed and place a clean sheet on top to give you a clear sorting surface to work on. Take any dirty clothing to the laundry and bring any clean clothing belonging to that bedroom back with you. Better still, bring the washing and ironing totally up to date prior to organising your bedrooms. If you have a portable clothes rack or an over-the-door laundry holder, now is the time to get them out. Have an additional box in which to store old wire coathangers which, hopefully, after your wardrobe workout, will be replaced by a new set of good quality coathangers. Once that's done, grab your notebook and let's get started!

 # Step 1: initi8

Note your frequent frustrations. Are your clothes squashed together in drawers or on shelves, requiring them to be ironed for a second time? Do you find it impossible to vacuum your walk-in wardrobe because of all the shoes and clutter on the floor? Do you often face the dilemma of trying to decide which clothes are clean and which are dirty among the piles in the bedroom corner? Maybe it's the time you waste searching through crowded racks of clothes but finding nothing you want to wear that frustrates you. Do you resent that extra 15 minutes wasted every morning, frantically racing around getting ready for work, knowing that it sets the tone for the rest of the day?

Set your vision and your goals, gather your tools and get in the mood.

> ## Note it!
>
> It's time to list your frequent frustrations and write your vision and your goals in your notebook. If you haven't already set up your organising kit, cleaning kit and tool kit, do it now.

Step 2: investig8

Physically, bedrooms contain both built-in and free-standing furniture such as beds, side tables, chests of drawers, wardrobes, chairs, lamps,

TVs, clocks and decorator items. They may also contain desks, gym equipment and toys. Bedrooms come in all shapes and sizes and furniture can be configured in a variety of ways. Bedrooms vary in the number of occupants, and they need to satisfy the requirements of each of them. Most of what is stored in bedrooms amounts to wardrobe items.

Functionally, bedrooms primarily provide for sleep. But many other functions are performed in this room, such as resting, dressing and undressing, reading, studying, romancing, playing, escaping and convalescing.

Emotionally, the bedroom has the most potential for personal expression. This room offers a lot of freedom in terms of decorating and organising to suit personal taste. A cluttered bedroom can emotionally cripple an occupant, but a bedroom can also be a real haven, a sanctuary and a very restful place if organised appropriately.

But pretty much, bedrooms are just one big wardrobe with a bed! So if we fix our wardrobes, the bedroom is finally free to fulfil its potential.

Note it!

What physical, functional and emotional elements need to be considered in your bedroom? Take a good look around the room and note anything that needs fixing or purchasing. Take measurements if you need to, and snap a few 'before' photos before getting into the 'Do it' phase.

 Step 3: consolid8

Sort your bedroom items into big fat categories. Lay out your sorting containers and group items together, throwing out as much as possible along the way. Here is a list of typical bedroom big fat categories with their subcategories. Use them or create your own:

- *underwear:* underpants, panties, girdles, bras, vests, singlets, spencers, camisoles petticoats, slips, pantyhose and socks
- *sleepwear:* pyjamas, nightdresses, robes and dressing gowns

- *outerwear:* coats, jackets, raincoats, skirts, trousers, jeans, shorts, shirts, blouses, T-shirts, tops, vests, jumpers, sweaters, cardigans, dresses and evening wear
- *footwear:* shoes, boots, sandals, slippers, runners, trainers, sand shoes, sports shoes, thongs and flip-flops
- *accessories:* handbags, briefcases, satchels, scarves, belts, watches, jewellery, ties, hats, handkerchiefs and gloves
- *sportswear:* casual, leisure, track pants, sweat tops, gym, swimwear, and specialist sports or team wear (such as ski or tennis gear)
- *travel items:* suitcases, overnight bags, toiletry bags and travel accessories (such as adapters, neck pillows and shoe bags)
- *linen items:* bed linen, blankets, comforters, bed spreads, pillows, under-blankets and mattress protectors (and maybe towels, face washers, bath mats and robes)
- *children's toys:* dolls, prams, dolls' houses, games, trucks and more
- *reading material:* books, magazines and catalogues.

Layer it!

As well as organising your items by type, as shown above, you may like to add a few extra layers to make your wardrobe really rock! You will already be doing this instinctively, but it still pays to have a look at your options before you begin the consolidation process. Additional layers include:

- *by person:* each person can have a separate section of wardrobe space
- *by season:* summer to winter, sleeveless to long-sleeved
- *by size:* small to large
- *by shape:* irregular to uniform
- *by fabric:* light/delicate to heavy/sturdy, stretchy, lacy
- *by length:* short to long
- *by function:* work wear, uniforms, school wear, sportswear, evening wear, casual wear, gardening clothes
- *by colour:* light colours to dark colours of any item.

Multi-layer it!

Feel free to combine as many layers as you like. For example, if you wear a uniform to work, you might like to bring all uniform items together. Have a drawer, shelf and hanging section just for uniform items, making it easy to dress in the morning, instead of rummaging around all over the place. This works particularly well for children's school uniforms. Perhaps you should separate your T-shirts into a number of locations. You may put a few on a shelf together with your gym wear, a couple together with your gardening or painting clothes and perhaps one to keep with your swimwear. Once you get the hang of it you will have lots of fun discovering what works best for you.

Note it!

Make a list of your big fat categories and subcategories and create new ones as you discover things along the way.

Chunk it down

Work drawer by drawer, shelf by shelf until the entire bedroom contents are in their categories. Be ruthless with anything that has just been hanging around, unused and unloved. In such limited primary space everything must earn its right to stay. The entire bedroom should take you about a day to fully reorganise.

CAUTION

I strongly suggest you work on one big fat category or sub-category at a time, so you don't end up with your entire wardrobe dumped onto the bed. For example, go through all your coats and jackets, then your skirts, then your trousers, then your tops and so on. It's much easier and more time efficient. And should you need to stop for any reason you will be able to sleep soundly in your bed!

Remember that you can do just one subcategory any time you have a spare eight minutes. Just set the timer and go, go, go!

Dora delves into her drawers and gets her knickers out of their knot!

Dora's underwear drawer was full to the brim. Her goal was to organise this drawer within 15 minutes, so she set her timer, popped on some music, grabbed her water bottle, cleaning kit and tool box and got straight to work. She placed six clean shoe boxes on her bed labelled bras, undies, pantyhose and socks, petticoats and slips, vests and singlets, and another with 'Not Underwear' written on it. She had her rubbish bin and her charity box nearby ready for work. It only took her a couple of minutes to empty the jumbled contents of her underwear drawer into the labelled shoe boxes. She methodically went through each box eliminating what she no longer wanted and neatly placed what she was keeping back into the shoe boxes. She cleaned out the drawer and placed boxed and sorted underwear into the drawer.

Everything was organised, she could see everything she had at a glance and dressing would be easy. She also decided it was time to purchase some new underwear as she was short on some of the basics. So she noted this on the shopping list page of her notebook. She also considered purchasing some drawer dividers but decided that the shoe boxes would be good enough until she had organised the entire room. Luckily, she remembered that shopping for containers comes last. Dora glanced at her timer and noted the time spent in her notebook: 14 minutes! She finished with time to spare!

Step 4: elimin8

Eliminate as much as you can by asking the following critical questions of each item you are unsure about:

- Do I wear you? If so, how often? When was the last time? When will be the next time?

- Do I need you? Do you go with other items in my wardrobe?
- Do I really want you? Do you suit and flatter my current body shape?
- Do I love you? Do I receive compliments when I wear you?

Create a working wardrobe

Fashions change, your body shape changes, your job changes and your lifestyle changes, so why are the same old clothes hanging around in your wardrobe? Think about who you are, what you do and how you want to present yourself to the world. By releasing your unflattering or hardly worn garments, you can create a wardrobe that works: one that's easy to dress from and that makes you feel and look good, regardless of where you need to go or what you need to do. The things you release will have a new life elsewhere and you will have a new lease of life as well!

Create a capsule wardrobe

This is a term used to describe a way of putting clothing together to form outfits that mix and match. Capsule wardrobes see clothing as sets rather than as individual pieces. If you create a few capsules you can vary the way you dress with fewer pieces of clothing. Follow these steps and create a few capsules of your own:

- Choose three bottoms—maybe a pair of jeans, a pair of pants and a basic skirt. Your three bottoms must go together and not clash with each other. Lay them out on the bed to check. You wouldn't choose a green, blue and purple skirt!
- Choose seven tops that match with all of your bottoms— maybe a singlet, a couple of plain T-shirts or shirts, a patterned shirt or T-shirt, an evening top, a jacket, a coat, a vest, a sweater, a jumper or a cardigan. The key is that not only must all the tops match all the bottoms, all the tops must also go together. Lay them out and they should not clash with each other.
- You should now be able to create up to 30 outfits from this capsule. Because every bottom works with every top and the tops work well together, you only need to get creative.

Put one bottom on and then maybe the singlet, followed by a shirt with the jacket or cardigan for extra warmth. All the pieces should work together in layers and separately. Accessorise with scarves, belts and jewellery. Add shoes and a handbag and you are set to go.

- Create a few capsules: one for going to work, one for staying at home, one for general out-and-about wear, one for leisure or gym time and one for travel. Some items can belong to more than one capsule, such as jeans and basic black or white tops or bottoms.
- Try all the combinations on and take photos to remind yourself of how they look.

Partner up

While you are deciding on what stays and what goes, you will discover items you love, but have never worn. It could be that you still love them and want to wear them but you don't have other pieces to go with them. For example, you may have a great skirt but no top to wear with it. We refer to that skirt as being unattached and your job is to find a partner for it. So take it shopping to find a top or jacket to turn it into a perfect match!

Your limits will set you free

Set limits on what will be stored in primary and secondary bedroom storage space and how much you want in secondary storage space elsewhere. How many T-shirts, skirts, black trousers, jackets, scarves, handbags, shoes or underpants are enough? Consider the amount of storage you have and the users of the room.

On the catwalk

Much of what you eliminate will be no-brainers, but there will be some items that you will agonise over. So rather than agonise over items in doubt now, give them one last chance. Create a 'fashion parade' container and place items in doubt into it. After you have finished organising the rest of your wardrobe, put your makeup on, do your hair and have a 'family and friends' fashion parade to decide on what stays and what goes. Give each member of your audience a piece of paper with KEEP IT written on one side and LOSE IT on the other side. Get them to hold their sign up as you prance and parade in your doubtful garments and let democracy take its course — majority rules!

Step 5: alloc8

Allocate containers and locations for what you are keeping. The advantage now is that you can see exactly how much stuff and space you have. The trick is to match the stuff with the space. If you still have clothing in the laundry awaiting washing or ironing, be sure to allow space for it when it returns to the wardrobe. Better still, bring the washing and ironing totally up to date prior to organising your bedroom.

Organise your bedroom by allocating space by person, by function (such as work clothing or sports clothing), or by type or shape of item (such as scarves, long tops, short tops, dresses or trousers). The choice is yours, and you can combine them. Do whatever makes sense to you.

Note it!

How are you going to allocate the space in your bedroom? Do you prefer to organise by person, by function, by type or shape of item, or by a combination of these?

Consider everybody's needs, look at what you are working with and make a decision. Measure the space and decide on the containers that best suit.

Storage smarts for bedrooms

Refer to masterclass 4: getting a handle on hardware for a quick refresher, if necessary. When organising the bedroom consider the amount of storage space you have and your priorities.

Following are some guidelines for bedroom storage.

An undercover affair

Organise your underwear:

- When you find a pair of undies you love, buy as many pairs as you need in a typical week and then add a couple of spares. As they start to wear out, in a year or so, find another pair you love and repeat the process. Do the same with bras, camisoles, singlets and so on. Remember your shape, your needs and your taste will change, so don't purchase too much of anything.

- Keep 'special occasion' undies separate from your day-to-day wear. Zip-lock bags work really well for these.

- Place rolled-up pantyhose or tights of the same type and colour in zip-lock bags or containers. Dressing will be a dream without the annoyance of rummaging through tangled tights and hosiery.

- Dispose of hosiery with ladders or holes immediately. Or place slightly imperfect hosiery in a separate zip-lock bag for wearing under trousers for extra warmth in winter.

- Keep socks in their pairs, rolled up or folded over.

- Keep socks of like colour grouped together, for ease of dressing.

- Place socks into containers in drawers. Shoeboxes are a great divider to start with.

- Once you like a pair of socks, purchase a few pairs so that matching them is easier.

- If you have a lone sock box, match up the pairs and cull regularly.

Pyjama party

Organise your sleepwear:

- Hang dressing gowns and robes on hooks in the bathroom or bedroom. This item is likely to be the longest garment in your wardrobe, but it's silly to have a hanging rod set at a height for just one or two garments. It's better to fold robes not in use and hang the one being worn on a hook for airing between uses.

- Cull your sleepwear down to a few favourites, send the rest to charity and rotate the ones you wear so they all stay fresh and feel nice on the skin.

- If you feel the need to have a couple of sets of sleepwear for travel or for hospital, pop these into zip-lock bags and place them on the bottom of the sleepwear drawer or shelf.

It's a cover up
Organise your outerwear:

- Wire hangers get entangled and are notorious for causing hanger stretch marks! Use a uniform set of good quality hangers, in one colour, to give your wardrobe an instant lift. A good, solid, general purpose, plastic hanger is great for hanging most items such as T-shirts, shirts, tight knits, light jackets and dresses—but not trousers. The weight of trousers is usually too much

A dream wardrobe with space for everything

for the strength of the middle bar on a typical plastic hanger and it will end up bowing. This causes your trousers to wrinkle at the fold, making them unsuitable to wear until you iron out the wrinkles.

- Face items in one direction for easy selection.
- Coats, jackets and raincoats should be hung on heavy-duty suit hangers and covered, when out of season, to protect them from shoulder dust and fading.
- Hang skirts on skirt hangers, one skirt per hanger.
- Hang trousers on skirt hangers, trouser clamps or trouser hangers, and only one item per hanger.
- Jeans and shorts can be hung, or folded and placed on a shelf.
- Shirts and blouses should have the top button done up to prevent them from slipping off the hangers and to keep collars and shoulders straight and in line.

- T-shirts, tops and vests benefit from hanging if you have the space. If they are folded, consider using a garment folder to keep everything uniform and looking neat.

- Jumpers, sweaters and cardigans with a tight knit can be hung on padded hangers. Those with a loose knit should be folded and placed in drawers or on shelves.

- Eveningwear should be folded and boxed to keep it from sagging, catching, fading and getting dusty and dirty. Wrap it in tissue, place it in a box and store it on a top shelf.

- Loose, textured garments or items with beading, such as tops or dresses, hang out of shape and should be folded on shelves or placed in boxes to protect them.

- Allow breathing space between garments. Only one item should be hung on a hanger—don't double up!

- Use garment protectors to protect expensive, infrequently worn or out-of-season clothing from dust and light.

- Air items before replacing them in the wardrobe.

Kick up your heels
Organise your footwear:

- Shoes can be stored in a variety of ways: on shelves or in drawers, heel to heel, toe to heel and one in front of the other. Each has its own advantages. Heel to heel lets you see both shoes facing the front or the back, heel to toe gives you a little bit of extra space where needed. One in front of the other works for deep shelves: you select the one in the front and reach behind for its mate.

- Shoes can go on shoe rails or racks, in wall cupboards, in drawers or on hanging shelving. You can use additional storage in other rooms

Shelf storage for shoes

as well. I have seen many shoe lovers dedicate whole storage cupboards to their shoe collection!

- Store boots in boot boxes on shelves and keep them in shape with rolled-up newspaper stuffed inside them.
- If you have lots of sports shoes and minimal storage, place them in a container and store them on shelves.

Dress it up
Organise your accessories:

- Good handbags usually come with bags to store them in. Store them in the bags, label them with the bag's description and place them on a shelf. Stuff bags with newspaper if they need some support to keep their shape.
- Roll scarves up and place them in containers in a drawer or hang them through hoops. Try using multi-level trouser hangers to hang lots of scarves without taking up much space.
- Belts can be hung from hooks on the sides of cupboards or you can purchase special-purpose belt holders. They may also be rolled up and placed in shallow drawers.
- Hats can be stored in hat boxes and caps can be stacked together. Both can be stored on shelves.
- Gloves can be stored in a container in a drawer.
- Watches and jewellery can be stored in shallow drawers fitted with jewellery dividers, in hanging jewellery organisers or in fishing tackle boxes. Try putting your earrings in ice-cube trays—they work really well. Of course, there are lots of special-purpose jewellery organisers, boxes and rolls that you can use.
- Noticeboards with hooks can work really well for hanging necklaces.

Hot and sweaty
Organise your sportswear:

- If you regularly attend a gym, play a sport or go swimming, have a bag dedicated to each activity. Keep all your gear in your bag ready to go. Place the bag on a hook by the front door or put it straight in the car the night before.

- Leisure wear can be folded on a shelf, put into drawers or hung on hanging rods. Keep this category sectioned off from the rest of your clothing.

Bon voyage!
Organise your travel items:

- If you travel frequently, consider having a toiletry bag permanently packed with small-sized toiletries. You can also pack almost-finished tubes of toothpaste, shampoo, conditioner and creams to use on your trips and throw them away before returning home.

- Store suitcases stacked inside each other where possible. Place a tag on the handle of the largest bag showing its contents.

- Keep your travel accessories in a container or a bag and place it inside your smallest suitcase or on a shelf, according to your frequency of use. Keep a list of the contents on file and label the container.

Use an over-the-door hanger to organise your travel wear before packing

Tuck me in
Organise your linen items:

- Store sheet sets in their pillowcases on shelves.

- Towels should be folded with the fold facing the front.

- Extra bedding not currently in use can be placed in vacuum bags to reduce the amount of space required. Place it on top shelves until needed.

Step shelf to the rescue!

- Bed and bath linen is often stored in bedrooms to free up space elsewhere or just to have items close to where they are being used. (Linen is covered in more detail in chapter 7: laundry hung and dried.)

Child's play
Organise your children's toys:

- Children's toys often occupy a large part of their bedrooms. This room needs to be kept in balance so that the activities of sleeping, reading, homework and playing are all supported but none dominate.
- Use containers to store toys and keep them on shelves, in cupboards or in living spaces.
- Label containers with words or pictures to identify the contents.
- Cull, cull, cull and limit, limit, limit the toy department. Every toy you keep is another toy to put away and away and away! (Toys are covered in more detail in chapter 10: fresh faces for living spaces.)

Read all about it
Organise your reading material:

- Lots of people read in bed, but the room doesn't need to be littered with a library full of books. One or two reading items popped on a bedside table looks and feels great. A big stack of books is overwhelming and makes for nightmares instead of sweet dreams.
- Have a reading department by your bedside in a drawer or in a box on the night stand. Add a pen and a small notebook for those flashes of brilliance that pop into

Create a bedside reading zone

your head in the middle of the night! Have some sticky notes for bookmarking information and comments, your reading glasses and a book light or a good lamp nearby. Finish it off with a cosy reading pillow! Your bedroom reading station is now complete. (Books are covered in more detail in chapter 10: fresh faces for living spaces.)

Don't give an inch

With some handy measurements for space allocation, you'll have a better idea of how much hanging or shelf space you need, how much of that can be doubled up (a row of short items such as jackets hung over another row of short items such as skirts), how much you need for long garments such as dresses and skirts, and how much shelf space you'll need for jumpers, sweaters, knits and shoes. Here are some measurements to get you started.

- Suits, jackets and bathrobes take up 5 to 10 centimetres of hanging rod length.
- Shirts, skirts and trousers take up 2.5 to 5 centimetres of hanging rod length.
- Dresses take up 2.5 to 7.5 centimetres of hanging rod length.
- Overcoats and outerwear jackets take up 10 to 15 centimetres of hanging rod length.
- Jumpers or sweaters which, like most knits, should be folded rather than hung, are 25.5 to 35.5 centimetres deep when folded and take up about 30 centimetres of shelf space.
- T-shirts and turtlenecks take up 22.5 to 25.5 centimetres of shelf space.
- Folded shirts take up 22.5 centimetres of shelf space.
- Pairs of women's shoes take up 18 to 20.5 centimetres of shelf space.
- Pairs of men's shoes take up 20.5 to 25.5 centimetres of shelf space.

These measurements are approximate and assume items are hanging freely and not all squashed together. Items take less space if they are crammed together, but are much harder to remove and replace and often require additional ironing.

Step 6: activ8

Finish it all off and put everything in its place:

- Give the bedroom a thorough clean, including light fittings. Your bedroom should look like the ones you admire in magazines: fresh, clean and welcoming.
- Place items into their new locations, adjusting and adding storage if necessary. Label containers.
- Decide how much you want to have out on surfaces. Aim for the least amount possible. Items on bedroom surfaces take up valuable working space.
- Lastly, add a few decorator accessories to give the room your personal touch.

Step 7: evalu8

Well done—you've finished the 'Do it' phase! You can now stand back and admire your results and measure them against your vision and the goals you set for yourself. It's time to get your camera out to take your 'after' photos. Compare them with your 'before' photos. *Wow!* What a difference! Go back to the notes you took in the 'Plan it' phase and note your answers to the following questions.

Note it!

- Have your frequent frustrations been addressed?
- Have you achieved your vision and your goals?
- Does your bedroom physically, functionally and emotionally please you?

If you say 'no' to any of these questions, make adjustments now or make a note to follow up within seven days. Continue to evaluate your bedroom and make changes as your lifestyle and circumstances change.

 Step 8: celebr8

No bedroom is going to keep itself looking the way yours does right now. You need to add regular bedroom cleaning and maintenance to your home care schedule. So let's quickly make a list of the tasks that need to be done to keep your bedroom humming. Here is an example of timely tasks for bedrooms. Use this list or create your own.

Timely tasks for bedrooms

Daily	Weekly	Monthly	Quarterly
Make bed like a five-star hotel	Vacuum or wash floors	Clean windows	Tidy wardrobe and declutter cupboards
Remove clutter	Dust surfaces and mirrors	Clean bedroom cupboards	Clean blinds or curtains
Hang clothes or take to laundry	Change bed linen	Rotate mattress	Refresh bedroom with a new look and feel

Lock it in!

Once you have completed your own task list, add the tasks to your home care schedule. You will need to lock in a time to complete each task to maintain your new-look bedroom.

Raise the bar!

It's time to set new standards, new rules and new rituals to maintain your clean, organised and functional bedroom.

Keep your 'before' and 'after' photos handy to remind yourself of how far you have come and to see the new standard you have set. Create a few new rules such as: 'I never leave dirty cups and glasses on the bedside table', 'I make my bed as in a five-star hotel' and 'I do an in8minute tidy-up every morning before leaving the room'.

String a few tasks together to create a few new rituals. Your bedtime bedroom ritual could be something like this:

- Set the timer and, in8minutes or less, make bed, put clothing away and clear any clutter.
- Take dirty washing to the laundry.

I bet you will have time to spare!

Create new rituals to guide you through holiday preparation and packing, and any other stressful time periods or tasks.

Maintain it!

Now all you need to do is follow your home care schedule and live up to your new standards. It will be easy to achieve with your fresh, clean bedroom as your foundation.

> **Note it!**
>
> I have completed my timely tasks for bedrooms and locked times into my home care schedule.
> My new rules are: _____
> My new rituals are: _____

Congratulations! It's time to celebrate. You did it! You have created a bedroom that is clean, organised and functional. It's time to collect your reward for completing this room. Book in a massage, have coffee with friends, go to a show or just have a bath! You deserve it!

Are you ready for another room? Then turn to the relevant page and motor on!

10

Fresh faces for living spaces

> Children always know when company is in the living room — they can hear their mother laughing at their father's jokes.

Anon

Let me entertain you

'We're having a party. Are you coming?'

'I can't wait to get home to snuggle up under a blanket and watch a movie. Hey, where's the remote control?'

'Come on in. Dinner's nearly ready!'

'Do you want to come over to watch the game on the big screen?'

All these questions and statements refer to the day-to-day activities that take place in our living spaces: family rooms, living rooms, dining rooms, billiard rooms, games rooms, rumpus rooms and entrances. They have many names, but they are all living spaces. They bring people together for relaxation and recreation, fun and games, wining and dining, and parties and entertaining. These spaces are also public places. This means that they are often not as disorganised as other areas of the home, due to the occasional frenzied clean-up they receive at the approach of visitors! Together we'll create clean, organised and functional living spaces that you'll be proud to share with your family and friends.

Now read on and I'll reveal the **in8steps** system checklist for creating fresh faces for your living spaces.

in8steps at a glance

Tick the boxes as you complete the steps for living spaces.

 Step 1: initi8 the process

☐ Identify your frequent frustrations.

☐ Set your vision and your goals.

☐ Gather your tools: set up your organising, cleaning and tool kits.

☐ Get in the mood: dress for success, turn up the music and have refreshments on hand.

 Step 2: investig8 what you have

☐ Note the physical, functional and emotional elements.

☐ Draw a floor plan and take measurements as required.

☐ Discover what's in your cupboards, on shelves and in drawers. Get an overview.

☐ Note anything you need to purchase or fix.

☐ Take 'before' photos.

 Step 3: consolid8 into big fat categories

☐ Set up 'Bin it', 'Gift it', 'Sell it' and 'Move it' containers.

☐ Determine your big fat categories and subcategories.

☐ Sort everything into big fat categories and subcategories.

 Step 4: elimin8 what you don't use, need, want or love

☐ When in doubt about an item, ask it the critical elimination questions:

— Do I use you? If so, how often? When was the last time? When will be the next time?

— Do I need you? Could I borrow you or substitute you with something else?

— Do I really want you or just the memory of you or where you came from? To preserve the memory, take a photo!

— Do I love you? Are you of sufficient sentimental value for me to keep?

☐ Set limits for both primary and secondary storage using number, space and date as a guide.

☐ Release it! Bin the trash, gift items to charity or friends, sell items of value and move things back to their correct rooms or to secondary storage.

 Step 5: alloc8 containers and locations for what you are keeping

☐ Purchase any new storage components you need. Recheck measurements first.

☐ Allocate storage space and make any necessary adjustments.

Step 6: activ8 your space

☐ Thoroughly clean the room, including all storage surfaces and interiors.

☐ Adjust or install storage components as necessary.

☐ Place items into their new containers and locations.

☐ Label containers, shelves and drawers as appropriate.

Step 7: evalu8 how it's working

☐ Have your frequent frustrations been addressed?

☐ Have you achieved your vision and your goals for this space?

☐ Does the room physically, functionally and emotionally please you?

☐ Make adjustments and finetune the system until it's running smoothly.

☐ Take 'after' photos.

Step 8: celebr8 your success and maintain the system

☐ Create a list of tasks needed for regular cleaning and maintenance.

☐ Lock your tasks into your home care schedule.

☐ Raise the bar and set new standards, new rules and rituals.

☐ Congratulations! It's time to celebrate. You did it!

☐ Collect your reward. You certainly deserve it!

Before you begin

First, let's create a permanent home for all remote controls and TV guides. A basket, container or drawer can serve this purpose, as long as it's a dedicated place and will be used consistently, at least by you. Let other family members know, but until you find a way to totally control other family members, be content with knowing you have a place and that you, at least, will be using it. The others will follow along eventually if you go about it without being a boss or a martyr. Put the remote controls back into their new home, cheerfully and repeatedly, until the family gets the message. Don't nag, boss or tell. Don't even give them the 'look'. Just lead by example. Remember that this journey is about you and your stuff and that being organised is a gift to yourself.

Now clear all surfaces that can be used as sorting areas. Once that's done, grab your notebook and let's get started!

 # Step 1: initi8

Note your frequent frustrations. Does continually searching for the remote controls drive you crazy? Is the furniture littered with old newspapers and magazines? Are you embarrassed to invite friends over for a drink? Do you have so many ornaments that you can't cope with the dusting? It's time to give each living space a fresh face.
Set your vision and your goals, gather your tools and get in the mood.

Note it!

It's time to list your frequent frustrations and write your vision and your goals in your notebook. If you haven't already set up your organising kit, cleaning kit and tool kit, do it now.

Step 2: investig8

Physically, living spaces are the most spacious areas of the home. They are filled with furniture, bookcases, sofas, cupboards, tables, chairs, rugs, lamps and entertainment equipment such as TVs and sound systems. Books, videos, CDs, DVDs, games and ornaments complete the picture. They often hold all the 'good' stuff: the good china, the good glassware and the good cutlery for guests. Their relative size sometimes attracts items that don't belong in them, just because of the availability of space—especially in corners where a junk pile is sometimes forced to wear a tablecloth so it can pretend it's a piece of furniture!

Functionally, living spaces focus on leisure and celebrations. They bring people together for relaxation and recreation, fun and games, wining and dining, and parties and entertaining. People spend time in living spaces studying, doing homework, listening to music, pursuing hobbies, doing crafts, exercising, watching movies and TV, writing letters or simply dozing off. They are sometimes used as guest rooms when friends sleep over after a late night. And there is more—too much to list. But you get the picture: lots of activities are undertaken in living spaces, so you need to consider them all.

Emotionally, living spaces put on the public face of the home. You want this room to feel and look good for family and friends. Use colour, lighting, furnishings and decorator items to express those feelings.

Note it!

What physical, functional and emotional elements need to be considered in your living space? Take a good look around the room and note anything that needs fixing or purchasing. Take measurements if you need to, and snap a few 'before' photos before getting into the 'Do it' phase.

Step 3: consolid8

Sort your living-space items into big fat categories. Lay out your sorting containers or use surfaces to group items together, throwing out as much as possible along the way. Here is a list of typical living spaces big fat categories with their subcategories. Use them or create your own:

- *entertainment:* games, movies, music, remote controls and TV guides
- *reading:* magazines, articles, newspapers, catalogues and books
- *entertaining:* crockery, cutlery, glassware, platters and vases
- *photos:* prints, negatives, albums and digital photos on media storage devices
- *hobbies and crafts:* stamp collecting, coin collecting, photography, sewing, knitting and scrapbooking
- *collections:* spoons, ornaments and general collectables
- *children's toys:* games, puzzles, building blocks, dolls and trucks
- *transit items:* keys, glasses, handbags, wallets, mobile phones, coats, hats, umbrellas, shoes and schoolbags.

Note it!

Make a list of your big fat categories and subcategories and create new ones as you discover things along the way.

Chunk it down

Work drawer by drawer, shelf by shelf until the entire living-space contents are sorted. Be ruthless with anything that has just been hanging around, unused and unloved. In such primary space everything must earn its right to stay. The entire living space should take you a few hours to fully reorganise. Remember that you can do just one subcategory any time you have a spare eight minutes. Just set the timer and go, go, go!

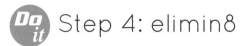 Step 4: elimin8

Eliminate as much as you can by asking the following critical questions of each item you are unsure about:

- Do I use you? If so, how often? When was the last time? When will be the next time?
- Do I need you? Could I use something else as a substitute, or borrow you?
- Do I really want you or just the memory of you or where you came from? To preserve the memory, take a photo!
- Do I love you? Are you of sufficient sentimental value for me to keep?

Set limits on what will be stored in primary and secondary storage space and how much you want in secondary storage space elsewhere. How many CDs, DVDs, books and toys are enough? Consider the amount of storage you have and the users of the living space.

 Step 5: alloc8

Allocate containers and locations for what you are keeping. The advantage now is that you can see exactly how much stuff and space you have. The trick is to match the stuff with the space.

Organise your living space by allocating space by person, by function (such as game playing, reading or entertaining), or by type or shape of item (such as crockery, glassware, books or games). The choice is yours, and you can combine them. Do whatever makes sense to you.

Note it!

How are you going to allocate the space in your living areas? Do you prefer to organise by person, by function, by type or shape of item, or by a combination of these? Consider everybody's needs, look at what you are working with and make a decision. Measure the space and decide on the containers that best suit.

Diana's dining dilemma

For the last year Diana's dining room was totally covered in photos, craft paper, ribbons, tools, albums, scissors and cutters. It looked more like a disorganised scrapbooking shop than a dining room in a home. It was time to face her dining dilemma, reclaim the space and entertain again! Diana realised that while her hall closet was rarely used for coats, it would make a perfect craft storage solution. She set about sorting all her craft components and worked out that with the addition of six shelves and an assortment of containers she could customise the closet to accommodate her every craft and scrapbooking need. With her dining dilemma solved, she knew she could invite friends over without compromising her love for scrapbooking and her crafts. With the hall closet conversion nearby, the dining room could now be used for both crafting and entertaining!

Storage smarts for living spaces

Refer to masterclass 4: getting a handle on hardware for a quick refresher, if necessary. When organising living spaces consider the amount of storage space you have and your priorities.

Here are some guidelines for living-space storage.

The games people play

Let's look at how to organise your entertainment items.

Games

- Keep favourite games together in one location to make them easy to find.
- Place board games in boxes on their sides vertically, if you can, or neatly stack them so you can easily remove and replace one without disturbing the others. Place them directly on shelves, in a container or in drawers. Use small zip-lock bags to contain small game pieces, label them and place them in the

box. Secure boxes with rubber bands or string if the contents are inclined to spill out. Secure corners with tape if boxes are coming apart.

- Electronic games often come with devices to hold and stand on while playing them. Keep all the parts for each device together in one labelled container. Label all the little parts so you can easily fit the correct bits and pieces together and put them away again. Many an important attachment has been tossed away because no-one knew what it belonged to!

- Cards and small games should be placed vertically in boxes so any deck or game can be easily removed. Use rubber bands or string to secure cards that don't have boxes.

Movies

- Movies with covers can be stored by title or by type—for example, children's movies, thrillers, comedies or documentaries. You can number them and create an index so you can easily find the title you want. Store them on shelves or in containers on shelves, with the spines facing out for easy identification.

- There are many storage units available for movies and the type you use will depend on décor, space, preferences, quantity and frequency of use. Store frequently used DVDs—for example, an exercise DVD you use every morning or your children's favourite movies—in primary storage, and less frequently used ones in secondary storage.

- For movies without a cover, consider using CD/DVD storage books. Slip each disc into a slot and turn the pages. You can number and index both the slot and the disc for extra ease of use. Keep your index on your computer and place a copy of the index on the front cover of your disc book as well.

Music

- Music in all forms can be organised by genre or artist, depending on your preference.

- Arrange your CDs in boxes on shelves.

- If you load your CDs onto your current electronic music device, you can release the originals for others to enjoy, while still enjoying the music yourself. If you decide you prefer to keep the original CDs of the music that you downloaded, store your collection in secondary storage, as they will most likely not be accessed very often.

Remote controls and TV guides

- Have one dedicated location for remote controls and the TV guide. It could be a dish, a basket, a box or a tray—just as long as it fits your remote controls and TV guide and is easily accessible.
- Encourage everyone to use the dedicated location and at the end of the day pack any strays away.

Turn over a new leaf!

To organise your reading material you will need to have a location where you can store it as well as a place where you can read it. You can set up a reading area by choosing your favourite chair and throwing in a rug if you like to curl up nice and cosy. Add extra lighting if necessary and have a table or piece of furniture by one side to hold your reading material, your glasses and a snack.

Now that you have your reading station all organised, let's organise the reading material.

Magazines

- Start by looking at all the types of magazines you collect. Categorise them as best you can. Then decide on how many issues you want in primary space and how many issues you might like to keep in secondary storage for reference. If you collect magazines based on your family's hobbies or interests, you might like to have six months in primary space and maybe the rest in secondary storage to free up primary space. The important thing is to set your limits by number, date or the space you want your magazines to occupy.
- Magazines are best stored in labelled magazine boxes. Choose boxes that suit your décor if they are on display.

- Keep the latest edition on a coffee table or by your reading station so you remember to read it.

Articles and clippings

- Everyone needs a system to manage articles and clippings. We are all guilty of clipping jokes, articles, diet plans and fashion tips from magazines. But what do you do with them?

- With scanners being so readily accessible in homes, why not scan them, label them and keep them in a folder on your computer called 'Magazine clippings and articles' (or a name of your choice)? This removes the need to physically file them.

- If you prefer to keep the article, then experiment with using display books to hold your various collections: one for home decorator ideas and another for children's craft ideas, or maybe you prefer to have just one as a general catch-all. The key is having somewhere to put them. Display books keep the articles clean, are easy to flick through and store neatly on shelves or in magazine boxes. Label the spine for easy identification. Once the book is full, use the 'one-in: one-out' technique for keeping your clippings in check (each time you put a new one in, take an old one out).

Newspapers

Newspapers are easy to store because you don't store them. You read them and ship them out! Pick a number and decide how many days' papers you want to keep in your living space. Aim for a low number such as one or two! Then use the 'one-in:one-out' technique to keep newspapers to their set limit. Place them in a basket or magazine holder or on a surface near where papers are read.

Catalogues

If you are an avid catalogue reader or collector, who am I to spoil your fun? Keep catalogues in a basket or box for a day or two. If you wish to purchase items, add them to your shopping list.

Books

- As books come in many shapes and sizes and cover many topics, they can be stored in a variety of ways, for example:

Create your perfect home library

  - *By subject or author.* Cluster together all books relating to the one subject or author, then adjust your shelves to suit.

  - *By height.* Simply go through your books and group them together by height. Then sort them by subject or author within the height groupings. This works very well for novels, as most are a standard size. To maximise storage space, adjust shelving to take just one size of book per shelf.

  - *By grouping them.* If you have a category of books that covers a range of sizes, simply place them all to one side of the shelves using as many shelf heights as there are book heights. So, if you collect gardening books you could dedicate the left side of three shelves to cater for the various heights of the books in your gardening collection. Your personal development book collection could be positioned on the same three shelves but to the right. Your eye will see the collection as a cohesive group, even though they are spread down three shelves.

- As a general rule, store tall books on the top and bottom shelves with smaller books in the middle.

- Oversized books are better stored and stacked in a horizontal position.

- Use book ends to stabilise books at regular intervals.

- Reference books such as your dictionary, thesaurus, atlas, the Bible, street directory and first-aid book can be kept in a section all of their own.

- Children's books should be stored down low within easy reach of children. Use boxes with the book spines facing up so children can easily pull the box of books out at reading time. Rotate the books to maintain interest.

Season to taste

While some people store their cookbooks in the kitchen, others store them in the office or in living spaces. Here are some tips for organising recipe books and recipes.

- Only have frequently used recipe books in your primary space. Use magazine boxes or bookends to keep them in check.

- Store infrequently used recipe books in secondary locations.

- If you have recipe books with only one or two recipes you regularly use, scan the recipes, print copies for your recipe folder and release the recipe book to a new life elsewhere. Someone else will enjoy the recipes you have never tried!

- Ditch your recipe books. Download recipes from the internet and keep the ones you love on file.

- Use stickers to number recipe books with narrow spines and keep a master index for easy reference.

- Create a recipe folder for your family's favourite tried and true recipes.

- Have a display book for recipes you might try one day. Place scanned and clipped recipes into the display book and keep this with your primary storage recipe collection.

- Once you try a recipe and like it enough to make it a regular, place the recipe into your family recipe folder or file.

- Use a cross-reference sheet for frequently used recipes. Simply create a sheet of paper with the name of the recipe, the book it comes from and the page it's on. That way you can simply look up your sheet to find that your orange cake recipe is on page 64 of your *Idiot's Guide to Orange Cake-Making* book.

Simply the best

Dining rooms and other living spaces often store crockery, cutlery and glassware for entertaining, or act as secondary storage for the kitchen.

Organise your entertaining items:

- Much of what you store in this space is considered to be the best you have, so a little care needs to be taken. Typically, items will be stored in sideboards or cupboards, many of which will have fixed shelving and little opportunity to add shelves. Step shelves can come into their own in this situation to create the extra layers you need to store the good stuff!

- Place crockery in stacks of the same item: large plates with large plates, bowls with bowls. Add step shelves or regular shelves to accommodate stacks.

- Place cups and other shallow bowl shapes on a tray that fits the cupboards and add a shelf to support the tray. Now you can retrieve the cups in one move. Top and tail them for a better fit if the rims are wider than the bases.

- Store glasses in their boxes if you still have them. Otherwise place them on shelves in soldier rows and top and tail them if necessary.

- Store cutlery in trays inside drawers, on shelves in cupboards or on step shelves.

- Platters can be put on platter racks. If you have the boxes, you can stack them up. If not, then add a few extra layers of shelves so you can take one platter at a time (if this is possible). Otherwise, simply stack the platters up in one section, knowing that you will need to juggle them a bit to get the one you want.

Shutter clutter!

Living spaces are often the places where families store their photos, but the following principles apply regardless of where your photo collection is stored. If you have a large number of unsorted printed photos you will need to work through them over an extended period of time. If you allow 6 to 12 months, the pressure will be off and you can take time each week to really enjoy this fun project of going down memory lane. Organise your photos only after you have the rest of your home in order. This is how to do it painlessly.

- Group your photos by the type of storage they are currently in. Put albums with albums, boxes with boxes, packs with packs, discs with discs and so on, taking care not to disturb sets of photos from the same pack, occasion or date.

- Place any photos that are already somewhat sorted onto shelves to get them out of the way.

- You should be left with a random collection of photos from everywhere. Get a few boxes that will fit standard-sized loose photos and photo packs and load the unsorted photos into the boxes until they are all standing up proudly and facing in one direction in their new homes. If you have a half-filled box, place some crumpled paper into the empty cavity to keep the photos stable and upright. Store these on shelves that are easily accessible. Label each box with a decade—for example, 'The 2010s', or 'The 2000s' or 'The 1990s'—regardless of what they contain. (Of course, use decades that you think the photos relate to.)

- Make some dividers out of paper or light cardboard. Cut them to fit the boxes so that they stand slightly above the photos. You will be using one for each year your photo collection covers, but don't write anything on them yet.

- Take one unsorted box off the shelf and select the first photo in the front. Try to identify the year it was taken. If you can't pinpoint the year, what about the decade?

- Once you do have an idea of the date, write that year or decade on a divider, place the photo behind the divider and place both into the back of the box of that decade.

- Repeat with each photo, placing the dividers into chronological order at the back of the boxes of the correct decade. Continue until all the boxes have photos sorted into years and are all in order. Some decades will have more photos than others, so adjust the labels on the front of the boxes accordingly.

- While you are identifying the photos, write details on the back with an instant drying archive pen to keep a record of the people and the occasion the photo shows.

- You can also keep a record of dates and events on a sheet of paper or on your computer. You might note the dates of birthdays, weddings, holidays and so on. This helps to put your photos into context and helps you identify dates of other photos because you will recognise the same hair style or clothing. This record becomes your family chronology of events and, if you like, you can use it to plan your albums.

- Create a 'Don't know' divider for photos you have no clue about. Don't linger on these now. Place your 'Don't know' divider with photos behind them in the back of one of your boxes. Once you have sorted the rest of your photos you will have a better context for re-checking your 'Don't know' photos and you will be surprised at how many you can identify using clues from the rest of your collection.

- Once you have fully sorted your unsorted photos, go to your albums and decide if you are happy with them or whether they need a good cull. You can integrate the photos back to the boxes if you prefer this type of storage.

- Store negatives in envelopes marked with the date and occasion.

- There is a lot of software that can easily manage digital photos. Ideally, use a generic one rather than the one that suits your camera. You may find that when you switch cameras you have problems loading photos onto the old software.

- Keep any media devices that store photos well labelled as to their contents.

On your hobby horse!

Make room for your hobbies. You might like to dedicate a cupboard to your hobby and craft items. Place items in containers as much as possible, so that sets of items are easy to remove, use and replace. Many hobby stores and craft suppliers have specialist storage for your bits and pieces, so check them out for the best fit. If you need things to go into the field, use portable storage so all your equipment is easily transportable.

Pass the plate

Organise your collection:

- Regardless of what you collect, you need to make space for your collection; otherwise it will make space for itself! Decide how much space you will allow your collection to occupy and build special shelving or storage to accommodate it. If you have an extensive collection you may need a room or two. Remember that everything is competing for space and do you really want to sacrifice your living spaces to your collections? The choice is yours. If you have lots of display items but little display space, think about rotating items just as they do in galleries. Change with the seasons and have a new look every three months!

- If you have valuable collections, they should be recorded on a database or spreadsheet for insurance and investment purposes. Always keep original paperwork, receipts and containers for collectables.

Don't toy with me!

Living spaces are often zones for children's paraphernalia, where children can play under the watchful eye of adults nearby.

Organise your toys:

- The general rule with toys is that the amount of toys children have must not exceed your capacity to store them. Children are often happy playing with anything. Sometimes a few pots and pans, a wooden spoon and a blanket over a table—better known as a secret cave—will entertain them for hours. Don't create a rod for your own back by keeping every toy your children have ever received over their lifetime. Your children get older and they outgrow their toys. Often it's the adults who have difficulty releasing their children's toys. Neither you nor your children will miss them.

- Keep toys together by type, in baskets or containers on shelves or in a cupboard. If you want them to stay that way, you will need to supervise play and packing away until the children get the hang of what goes where. Label the outsides of the boxes with words or pictures, or stick an example of the contents on the outsides for children to see: a block could go on the outside of the block box, a small doll on the doll box and a small truck on the truck box.

- Limit the number of items out at any one time. Just pick a number. Insist on packing-up time—maybe an in8minutes run-around a few times a day. Rotate toys when boredom sets in for you or the children!
- Toy mats can work well as you just need to pick up the mat and the toys are gathered up!
- Keep puzzle parts together by assigning each puzzle a colour. Simply upturn the puzzle, get a coloured marker pen and run the pen across the back of each puzzle piece as well as the backing board. Store each puzzle's pieces in a zip-lock bag and place it in a box. Keep the backing boards nearby. If two puzzles get mixed up, just turn the pieces over and separate them by colour.

Coming through!

Organise your transit items. Transit items are things such as keys, glasses, handbags, wallets, mobile phones, coats, hats, umbrellas, shoes and schoolbags that come in and out of the house repeatedly. Having dedicated places for these items will make leaving the house and coming back home a breeze.

Organise your transit items:

- Create a permanent location for each of these items.
- Coats, scarves, hats, handbags and umbrellas can go onto hooks inside a cupboard or on a wall, or on a freestanding coat rack.
- Shoes can be placed on a stand just inside the door, in a cupboard or under a bench.
- Keys can be hung on hooks.
- Wallets and mobile phones can go into a container on a bench or on top of the fridge.
- Schoolbags can go on hooks in a cupboard or be stored in children's bedrooms.

- If possible and necessary, have a pair of glasses in each room where reading is likely to take place. Otherwise, have one or two locations for glasses.

Do it Step 6: activ8

Finish it all off and put everything in its place:

- Give the living space a thorough clean, including light fittings. Your living space should look like the ones you admire in magazines: fresh, clean and welcoming.
- Place items in their new locations, adjusting and adding storage if necessary. Label containers.
- Decide how much you want to have out on surfaces. Aim for the least amount possible.
- Lastly, add a few decorator accessories to give the room your personal touch.

Review it Step 7: evalu8

Well done—you've finished the 'Do it' phase! You can now stand back and admire your results and measure them against your vision and the goals you set for yourself. It's time to get your camera out to take your 'after' photos. Compare them with your 'before' photos. *Wow!* What a difference! Go back to the notes you took in the 'Plan it' phase and note your answers to the following questions:

Note it!

- Have your frequent frustrations been addressed?
- Have you achieved your vision and your goals?
- Do your living spaces physically, functionally and emotionally please you?

If you say 'no' to any of these questions, make adjustments now or make a note to follow up within seven days. Continue to evaluate your living space and make changes as your lifestyle and circumstances change.

 # Step 8: celebr8

No living space is going to keep itself looking the way yours does right now. You need to add regular living-space cleaning and maintenance to your home care schedule. So let's quickly make a list of the tasks that need to be done to keep your living space humming. Here is an example of timely tasks for living spaces. Use this list or create your own.

Timely tasks for living spaces

Daily	Weekly	Monthly	Quarterly
Put remote controls away	Dust surfaces	Clean cushions and throw rugs	Tidy and declutter cupboards
Clear clutter	Clean ornaments	Vacuum or clean upholstery	Clean blinds or curtains
Hang coats, hats and handbags	Vacuum and Wash floors	Clean windows	Refresh with a new look and feel

Lock it in!

Once you have completed your own task list, add the tasks to your home care schedule. You will need to lock in a time to complete each task to maintain your new-look living space.

Raise the bar!

It's time to set new standards, new rules and new rituals to maintain your clean, organised and functional living space.

Keep your 'before' and 'after' photos handy to remind yourself of how far you have come and to see the new standard you have set. Create a few new rules such as: 'I always put remotes back in their place', 'I always throw newspapers out after two days' and 'I always hang my coat on the hook when I come in'.

String a few tasks together to create a few new rituals. Your evening living space ritual could be something like this:

- Do a quick tidy up: put reading material away and shoes away.
- Wash cups and glasses, put reading glasses away, and put phones back on their rechargers.

Ahhh, a calm room to come in to, instead of a chaotic room to avoid!

Create new rituals to guide you through parties and entertaining and any other stressful time periods or tasks.

Maintain it!

Now all you need to do is follow your home care schedule and live up to your new standards. It will be easy to achieve with your fresh, clean living space as your foundation.

> **Note it!**
>
> I have completed my timely tasks for living spaces and locked times into my home care schedule.
>
> My new rules are: _____
>
> My new rituals are: _____

Congratulations! It's time to celebrate. You did it! You have created a living space that is clean, organised and functional. It's time to collect your reward for completing this room. Book in a massage, have coffee with friends, go to a show or just have a bath! You deserve it!

Are you ready for another room? Then turn to the relevant page and motor on!

Office overhaul

> Organised crime in America takes in over $40 billion a year and spends very little on office supplies.
>
> *Woody Allen*

You be the CEO

Is your office space somewhere you can think, plan, be creative and run the household? Or is it a place you drag yourself into only when absolutely necessary? Does the mere mention of paperwork make you weak at the knees? Do you stumble around your office tripping over piles of paper and other stuff that has been purposely deposited there or accidently left behind? Does this room have the one door in the house that simply must be closed when you have company? Well, all that is about to change. Your home office should be a place where you can manage the family finances, where you can plan your next holiday adventure and where family members can surf the web and do research for education or fun. Together we'll create an office that is clean, organised and functional.

Your office may be a dedicated room called the 'office', an area in the kitchen, or a corner of the bedroom or dining room. Organising your office is a bit more involved than organising the other rooms of the house because of the added complication of paperwork. This needs to be controlled at the processing stage as well as at the filing stage, and I have the system to do just that!

Now read on and I'll reveal the **in8steps** system checklist for overhauling your office.

in8steps at a glance

Tick the boxes as you complete the steps for offices.

Plan it   Step 1: initi8 the process

- ☐ Identify your frequent frustrations.
- ☐ Set your vision and your goals.
- ☐ Gather your tools: set up your organising, cleaning and tool kits.
- ☐ Get in the mood: dress for success, turn up the music and have refreshments on hand.

Plan it   Step 2: investig8 what you have

- ☐ Note the physical, functional and emotional elements.
- ☐ Draw a floor plan and take measurements as required.
- ☐ Discover what's in your cupboards, on shelves and in drawers. Get an overview.
- ☐ Note anything you need to purchase or fix.
- ☐ Take 'before' photos.

Do it   Step 3: consolid8 into big fat categories

- ☐ Set up 'Bin it', 'Gift it', 'Sell it' and 'Move it' containers.
- ☐ Determine your big fat categories and subcategories.
- ☐ Sort everything into big fat categories and subcategories.

Do it   Step 4: elimin8 what you don't use, need, want or love

- ☐ When in doubt about an item, ask it the critical elimination questions:
  - — Do I use you? If so, how often? When was the last time? When will be the next time?
  - — Do I need you? Could I borrow you or substitute you with something else?
  - — Do I really want you or just the memory of you or where you came from? To preserve the memory, take a photo!
  - — Do I love you? Are you of sufficient sentimental value for me to keep?

☐ Set limits for both primary and secondary storage using number, space and date as a guide.

☐ Release it! Bin the trash, gift items to charity or friends, sell items of value and move things back to their correct rooms or to secondary storage.

Step 5: alloc8 containers and locations for what you are keeping

☐ Purchase any new storage components you need. Recheck measurements first.

☐ Allocate storage space and make any necessary adjustments.

Step 6: activ8 your space

☐ Thoroughly clean the room, including all storage surfaces and interiors.

☐ Adjust or install storage components as necessary.

☐ Place items in their new containers and locations.

☐ Label containers, shelves and drawers as appropriate.

Step 7: evalu8 how it's working

☐ Have your frequent frustrations been addressed?

☐ Have you achieved your vision and your goals for this space?

☐ Does the room physically, functionally and emotionally please you?

☐ Make adjustments and finetune the system until it's running smoothly.

☐ Take 'after' photos.

Step 8: celebr8 your success and maintain the system

☐ Create a list of tasks needed for regular cleaning and maintenance.

☐ Lock your tasks into your home care schedule.

☐ Raise the bar and set new standards, new rules and rituals.

☐ Congratulations! It's time to celebrate. You did it!

☐ Collect your reward. You certainly deserve it!

Before you begin

Before you start organising your office, you need to have some clear surfaces to work on. So pack up any unsorted piles of paperwork and non-paperwork items that are currently cluttering these areas. Place items into separate labelled boxes and put them to one side and out of your way for now. Wipe down your cleared surfaces, grab your notebook and let's get started!

 Step 1: initi8

Note your frequent frustrations. Are you sick to the stomach about paying late fees for overdue bills festering somewhere in the pile? Does a request for information give you a migraine with the thought of knowing just how long it will take to find what you need? Have you missed appointments with your dentist or attended the appointment on the wrong day? Are the unfiled piles of paperwork getting on your nerves and giving you depression? Is your sleep disturbed by nagging doubts about whether you've paid the insurance or not? Do you long for a clear and organised space where you can explore your dreams and be creative?

Set your vision and your goals, gather your tools and get in the mood.

> ## Note it!
>
> It's time to list your frequent frustrations and write your vision and your goals in your notebook. If you haven't already set up your organising kit, cleaning kit and tool kit, do it now.

 Step 2: investig8

Physically, offices vary enormously—from a desk in a corner to a spacious room. Offices require adequate lighting, a surface to work on, somewhere to sit and storage for books, files, paperwork in progress, supplies and office tools. They have furniture including desks, tables, chairs, filing cabinets, bookcases and cupboards. They need power, phone and internet connection points. Offices house lots of computer stuff including printers, laptops, PCs, scanners, fax machines, hard drives and all their accessories and cables. Then there's the paperwork, which should be filed but all too often floods floors and wallpapers walls! Because we have too much stuff for the storage space available, our offices suffer from obesity and are bursting at the seams.

Functionally, the office is the main place where paperwork is looked at, sorted, processed, filed, stored and shredded. Printing, faxing, emailing, working and studying are other major functions undertaken in this room. If these are done using a functional system, paper flows. Without a system, paper piles up and gives us office constipation, where lots of paper is coming in but nothing is going out!

Emotionally, office spaces are overwhelming if they are filled with clutter and unfinished business. When people feel overwhelmed they just want to curl up or run away. Your office should leave you feeling efficient, productive, supported and in control. It also needs your personal touch, using your decorative flair and stationery style.

Note it!

What physical, functional and emotional elements need to be considered in your office? Take a good look around the room and note anything that needs fixing or purchasing. Take measurements if you need to, and snap a few 'before' photos before getting into the 'Do it' phase.

Step 3: consolid8

Initially, it's more efficient to break your office into two distinct areas—non-paperwork and paperwork—because paperwork has its own special needs. By working with the non-paperwork first, you will be left with the best possible environment to organise your paperwork.

Lay out your sorting containers and group your non-paperwork items together, throwing out as much as possible along the way. Here is a list of typical non-paperwork big fat categories with their subcategories. Use them or create your own:

- *office tools:* calculators, hole punches, staplers, writing implements, tape, label maker and scissors
- *office supplies:* toners, refills, staples, paper, label-maker tape and stationery
- *cables:* cables for your electronic gadgets, rechargers and extension cables
- *equipment:* phones, faxes, printers, scanners and drives
- *books:* reference books, novels and organising books.

Note it!

Make a list of your big fat categories and subcategories and create new ones as you discover things along the way.

Chunk it down

Work drawer by drawer, shelf by shelf, area by area until every big fat category has been sorted. Be ruthless with anything that has just been hanging around, unused and unloved. In such limited primary space everything must earn its right to stay. The office space should take you a few hours to fully reorganise, while the paperwork may take anywhere from a day to a week depending on how much paperwork needs sorting. Remember that you can do just one subcategory any time you have a spare eight minutes. Just set the timer and go, go, go!

Paula purges her paperwork

Paula had been a paper 'piler' for years — pile upon pile upon pile grew precariously from the floor. Each pile started as a few innocent pieces of paper, which declared an open invitation for any and all paper to join in. Paula had had enough. She packed up her piles into boxes and could not believe the relief she felt just by seeing the floor again. She vacuumed, put all her other stuff away and got straight to work creating her Paper Flow stations, which only took her 20 minutes to set up. That was the easy part and she knew that the sorting was still to come. Tentatively she opened the first box and set the timer for an in8minute power burst to get her started. She took out a small stack of paper. She lined up her sorting magazine boxes. She pressed the timer start button. The race was on! One box down, two boxes down, she powered on until she was down to the last piece. She was on the winner's podium, the crowd was cheering! She had done in a morning what she had been thinking about for more than two years. It was easy, she felt like a winner and she looked at her sorting boxes and at her watch! She had three hours before the school run. Enough time to get them into order. One at a time she sorted them. Finances first — oh, do I have seven bank accounts? Utilities next — yeah, there's the phone bill I was looking for! Health next — goodness, here's three medical bills I haven't claimed, can't wait to collect! Vehicles, small receipts, interests, important documents and all the other sorting box contents all came together to reveal her life. By the end of the day, she had purged her paper and given her office the overhaul SHE deserved!

Step 4: elimin8

Eliminate as much as you can by asking the following critical questions of each item you are unsure about:

* Do I use you? If so, how often? When was the last time? When will be the next time?

- Do I need you?
- Do I really want you?
- Do I love you?

Set limits on what will be stored in primary and secondary office storage space and how much you want in secondary storage space elsewhere. How many computers, printers, discs, paperclips, pens or pencils are enough? How many years of bank statements, old tax returns, paid electricity bills, school newsletters or old birthday cards are enough? Give your paperwork a limit (for example, a 'use-by date', which can differ for each subcategory) according to your needs. Decide how much you want to keep and set your own limits on every subcategory.

Consider the amount of storage you have, your legal requirements for things such as tax and investments, and the users of the room.

 Step 5: alloc8

Allocate containers and locations for what you are keeping. The advantage now is that you can see exactly how much paper, stuff and space you have. The trick is to match your paperwork and the stuff with the space.

Organise your office by allocating space by person, by function (such as bill paying, shredding, reading and correspondence), or by type or shape of item (such as cables, lever arch folders or boxes). The choice is yours, and you can combine them. Do whatever makes sense to you.

Note it!

How are you going to allocate the space in your office? Do you prefer to organise by person, by function, by type or shape of item, or by a combination of these? Consider everybody's needs, look at what you are working with and make a decision. Measure the space and decide on containers that best suit.

Storage smarts for the office

Refer to masterclass 4: getting a handle on hardware for a quick refresher, if necessary. When organising your office, consider the amount of storage space you have and your priorities. The office is nearly all primary space so excess supplies may have to be stored elsewhere. Choose a location as near as possible to the office.

Here are some guidelines for office storage.

Non-paperwork

First, let's look at how to organise the non-paperwork in the office.

Office tools

Keep your best set of office tools, such as calculators, hole punches, staplers, writing implements, tape, scissors and label makers, in a box on the desk or in the top drawer. Any duplicates can be placed in boxes in other areas of the home or in a supplies box called 'Office supplies' to replace the ones in your tool box(es) as needed.

Office supplies

Keep toners, refills, staples, paper and label-maker tape in a supplies box in a cupboard or on a shelf.

Cables

To organise your electronic cables and battery chargers, label your cables to ensure you know what goes with what. There are several alternatives for storing cables:

*   Keep them in hanging organisers with a series of see-through pockets. Place them on the back of a door or hang them from a hook or rod in the office or in a cupboard nearby.
*   Place them in labelled zip-lock bags and put these in a box or pin them to a notice board.
*   Hang them on hooks on a noticeboard.
*   Keep them in a box with ties holding them tight.

Equipment

Place phones, faxes, printers, scanners and drives in the best location in terms of power, internet and phone points, or get an electrician to make any changes necessary to have things in the best location for your needs.

Books

Keep books you use frequently (such as reference books) close at hand and others (such as novels and organising books) on bookcases nearby or in other rooms.

After you have sorted these non-paperwork items, it's time to tackle your paperwork.

Climb on board the Paper Flow express

I developed the Paper Flow system to help people organise their paperwork and I felt that this area of people's lives was so important that I dedicated an entire book to the subject. The book I wrote with Brigitte Hinneberg is called *Paper Flow* (Wrightbooks 2011). The book takes you through the system step-by-step, section-by-section, and creates a

Your Paper Flow station.
Wouldn't you love an office like this?

seamless system for managing your paperwork. Paper Flow is a simple system, much like a railway network, with six dedicated stations and a Paper Flow schedule to keep it running smoothly. Following is a brief description of the system.

- *Paperwork boards the system at the 'In-tray' station.* Set up a container and a location for what we will now call your in-tray. Choose a basket on your office bench, a tray in your office or a bowl on a side table. The choice is yours, but do it now! This station is notorious for getting overcrowded so security systems need to be set in place. The new rule is that this station must be cleared regularly for cleaning, with a minimum of once a week.

- *Paperwork gets processed at the 'Recurring actions' station.* 'Recurring action' refers to the type of paperwork that hits your in-tray on a regular basis, such as bills, items to file, correspondence and invitations to answer. To set up your recurring action station take six manila folders of one colour and label them 'Bills to pay', 'Items to file' and so on, and sort them in a step file, filing cabinet or in a desk topper.

- *Projects await completion at the 'Projects' station.* Items that relate to projects stay in this folder until the project is completed. Place your projects paperwork into a few manila folders of a different colour from your recurring action folders. Label these files with the names of the projects you have on the go, such as the party you are planning or the conference you are attending. Transfer this to a larger folder or magazine box if the file outgrows its manila folder.

- *Paperwork that will be referred back to is placed in the 'Reference' station.* Once your paperwork is processed through the 'Recurring action' and 'Projects' stations, the paperwork you decide to keep needs to be filed in folders. Determine your big fat categories to label each folder. For example, 'Family and pet health' is a big fat category and you can use tabbed dividers for each subcategory, such as 'Immunisation details'.

- *Paperwork is shunted into storage at the 'Archives' station.* From now on archives will hold old paperwork that needs to be kept, but won't be referred to or added to very often. This type of paperwork should be stored in containers or folders on top shelves, backs of cupboards or storage outside your office.

- *Paperwork that has to leave the system waits at the 'Out' station.* This type of paperwork may go on to other people or simply age beyond its usefulness and need to be binned or shredded. Paper going to other people—such as forms you need to lodge or a letter to post—needs to move out of the office. A dedicated 'Out' bag is a great solution for items leaving the office. Hang an empty bag on the back of your office door or anywhere convenient to you. As soon as you have anything that needs to leave the office, place it in your 'Out' bag and then hang it on the handle of the door through which you need to leave the house, so you don't forget it.

The Paper Flow schedule is a weekly plan that lists all your paperwork tasks in one simple document. By following a schedule you will ensure that paper work can be completed in just one in8minute power burst per day. Following is an example:

Paper Flow	Weekly Schedule for Recurring Action Files

Day	Items to be completed every week without fail
Every Day	Complete correspondence
Monday	Empty in-tray Update contacts
Tuesday	Pay bills Move projects forward
Wednesday	Empty in-tray Make claims
Thursday	Move projects forward
Friday	Empty in-tray Go through reading material at the local cafe File paperwork
Saturday	Do some fun paperwork—sort recipes, photos or travel stuff!
Sunday	Day off or catch up on some pleasure reading

Paper Flow schedule

CAUTION

Filing cabinets are fraught with danger. They tend to store stagnant paperwork and often they are just cemeteries for deceased and unnecessary paperwork. So, if you are guilty of being the out-of-sight, out-of-mind filing cabinet type, consider ditching the filing cabinet and filing your paperwork in lever arch folders.

 Step 6: activ8

Finish it all off and put everything in its place:

- Give the office a thorough clean, including light fittings, lamps and printers, under desks and in among the cables. Your office should look like the ones you admire in magazines: fresh, clean and welcoming.

- Place items in their new locations, adjusting and adding storage if necessary. Label containers.
- Decide how much you want to have out on surfaces. Aim for the least amount possible. Items on office surfaces take up valuable working space.
- Finally, add a few decorator accessories to give the room your personal touch.

Review it Step 7: evalu8

Well done—you've finished the 'Do it' phase! You can now stand back and admire your results and measure them against your vision and the goals you set for yourself. It's time to get your camera out to take your 'after' photos. Compare them with your 'before' photos. *Wow!* What a difference! Go back to the notes you took in the 'Plan it' phase and note your answers to the following questions.

Note it!
- Have your frequent frustrations been addressed?
- Have you achieved your vision and your goals?
- Does your office physically, functionally and emotionally please you?

If you say 'no' to any of these questions, make adjustments now or make a note to follow up within seven days. Continue to evaluate your office and make changes as your lifestyle and circumstances change.

Review it Step 8: celebr8

No office is going to keep itself looking the way yours does right now. You need to add regular office cleaning and maintenance to your home care schedule. So let's quickly make a list of the tasks that need to be done to keep your office humming. Here is an example of timely tasks for offices. Use this list or create your own.

Timely tasks for offices

Daily	Weekly	Monthly	Quarterly
Clear clutter	Clean surfaces, equipment and floors	Check supplies like toners and label-maker tape	Tidy and declutter cupboards
Do your recurring actions	Empty bins	Clean windows, curtains and blinds	Refresh with a new look and feel

Lock it in!

Once you have completed your own task list, add the tasks to your home care schedule. You will need to lock in a time to complete each task to maintain your new-look office.

Raise the bar!

It's time to set new standards, new rules and new rituals to maintain your clean, organised and functional office.

Keep your 'before' and 'after' photos handy to remind yourself of how far you have come and to see the new standard you have set. Create a few new rules such as: 'I always pay my bills on Mondays' and 'I always do an in8 minute tidy-up after using the office'.

String a few tasks together to create a few new rituals. Your end-of-day office ritual could be something like this:

- Turn off the computer and other equipment.
- Pack up the desk and leave it clear of clutter.
- Shred documents, empty the bin and post the mail.

Create new rituals to guide you through tax time and any other stressful time periods or tasks.

Maintain it!

Now all you need to do to follow your home care schedule and live up to your new standards. It will be easy to achieve with your fresh, clean office as your foundation.

> ### Note it!
>
> I have completed my timely tasks for offices and locked times into my home care schedule.
>
> My new rules are: _____
>
> My new rituals are: _____
>
> I have completed my Paper Flow schedule and locked times in to process my paperwork.

Congratulations! It's time to celebrate. You did it! You have created an office that is clean, organised and functional. It's time to collect your reward for completing this room. Book in a massage, have coffee with friends, go to a show or just have a bath! You deserve it!

Are you ready for another room? Then turn to the relevant page and motor on!

12

Lifting the door on garages

> The doctor must have put my pacemaker in wrong. Every time my husband kisses me the garage door goes up.

Minnie Pearl

What's behind your garage door?

How often have you seen people park their cars in the driveway or on the street, while their junk is in the garage safely protected from the elements? The rain, the hail, the sunshine, the snow and the frost inflict their daily damage on expensive vehicles, causing them to fade and age before their time. But the old newspapers are snug and dry. Stacks of boxes, with unspecified contents, park proudly on the garage floor or on top of workbenches, totally unaware of the outside weather conditions. Old bicycles awaiting repair and footballs needing air patiently but comfortably wait and wait and wait.

Your garage is a very expensive storage area if all it is storing is junk. It's time to lift the door on the garage, face the problem head on and let your car back in! Together we will create a garage that is clean, organised and functional.

The garage may be one area of the home where you need some reinforcements.

Now read on and I'll reveal the **in8steps** system checklist for lifting the door on garages.

in8steps at a glance

Tick the boxes as you complete the steps for garages.

Step 1: initi8 the process

☐ Identify your frequent frustrations.

☐ Set your vision and your goals.

☐ Gather your tools: set up your organising, cleaning and tool kits.

☐ Get in the mood: dress for success, turn up the music and have refreshments on hand.

Step 2: investig8 what you have

☐ Note the physical, functional and emotional elements.

☐ Draw a floor plan and take measurements as required.

☐ Discover what's in your cupboards, on shelves and in drawers. Get an overview.

☐ Note anything you need to purchase or fix.

☐ Take 'before' photos.

Step 3: consolid8 into big fat categories

☐ Set up 'Bin it', 'Gift it', 'Sell it' and 'Move it' containers.

☐ Determine your big fat categories and subcategories.

☐ Sort everything into big fat categories and subcategories.

Step 4: elimin8 what you don't use, need, want or love

☐ When in doubt about an item, ask it the critical elimination questions:
   — Do I use you? If so, how often? When was the last time? When will be the next time?
   — Do I need you? Could I borrow you or substitute you with something else?
   — Do I really want you or just the memory of you or where you came from? To preserve the memory, take a photo!
   — Do I love you? Are you of sufficient sentimental value for me to keep?

☐ Set limits for both primary and secondary storage using number, space and date as a guide.

☐ Release it! Bin the trash, gift items to charity or friends, sell items of value and move things back to their correct places or to secondary storage.

 ## Step 5: alloc8 containers and locations for what you are keeping

☐ Purchase any new storage components you need. Recheck the measurements first.

☐ Allocate storage space and make any necessary adjustments.

 ## Step 6: activ8 your space

☐ Thoroughly clean the garage, including all storage surfaces and interiors.

☐ Adjust or install storage components as necessary.

☐ Place items in their new containers and locations.

☐ Label containers, shelves and drawers as appropriate.

 ## Step 7: evalu8 how it's working

☐ Have your frequent frustrations been addressed?

☐ Have you achieved your vision and your goals for this space?

☐ Does the garage physically, functionally and emotionally please you?

☐ Make adjustments and finetune the system until it's running smoothly.

☐ Take 'after' photos.

Step 8: celebr8 your success and maintain the system

☐ Create a list of tasks needed for regular cleaning and maintenance.

☐ Lock your tasks into your home care schedule.

☐ Raise the bar and set new standards, new rules and rituals.

☐ Congratulations! It's time to celebrate. You did it!

☐ Collect your reward. You certainly deserve it!

Before you begin

Before you start organising your garage, you will need some space, either inside or outside of it. If your car can still fit into your garage (ha!) taking it out should leave enough floor space to provide a good sorting area. If your car is always out in the elements, your garage is probably so cluttered that you will have to lift the garage door and sort your stuff out in the driveway or on the front lawn. So, pick a sunny day! Once that's done, grab your notebook and let's get started!

 # Step 1: initi8

Note each of your frequent frustrations. Is it that you have to brave the weather, loaded with groceries, getting from street parking to the front door? Is it the lack of work space available for doing the simplest of repair jobs? Are you losing fitness while your weightlifting equipment is buried under a pile of rubbish or do you cringe at the sight of old tricycles knowing that your two children are now at university?

Set your vision and your goals, gather your tools and get in the mood.

> ## Note it!
> It's time to list your frequent frustrations and write your vision and your goals in your notebook. If you haven't already set up your organising kit, cleaning kit and tool kit, do it now.

 # Step 2: investig8

Physically, garages tend to have little purpose-specific storage. They are often just four walls, a roof and a floor. When storage is put into these areas it's usually a random selection of leftovers from the home. An old cupboard here, a few shelves there, a fridge or two, some wooden boxes ... and so it grows and evolves without any rhyme or reason. Usually, lighting and power points are inadequate and garages are often not insulated, making them subject to extremes in temperature.

Functionally, the garage's primary goal is to protect vehicles from the elements. However, this space has many other functions. We can clean and repair our cars and other items. It can be used for exercising with the installation of some gym equipment. Clear workbenches provide space for hobbies and projects. We can even entertain there when it doubles as a party room, and of course the men can escape to the man cave to watch sport in peace.

But the garage most often fails as a functional storage area. It can be used as primary storage for a range of garage big fat categories and has huge potential as a secondary storage area for household items.

Emotionally, garages tend to be masculine or neutral and are not usually given much planning or attention. They are often a man's pride and joy where he can enjoy the simple pleasures of tinkering with tools and fixing things.

Note it!

What physical, functional and emotional elements need to be considered in your garage? Take a good look around and note anything that needs fixing or purchasing. Take measurements if you need to, and snap a few 'before' photos before getting into the 'Do it' phase.

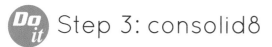 Step 3: consolid8

Sort your garage items into big fat categories. Lay out your sorting containers and group items together, throwing out as much as possible along the way. Here is a list of typical garage big fat categories with their subcategories. Use them or create your own:

- *vehicles:* motor bikes, boats, trailers, jet skis, spare parts and caravans
- *car-care products:* polishes, cleaning items, rags and sponges

- *tools:* power tools, hand tools, work clothing and ladders
- *painting equipment:* paint, rollers, brushes and accessories
- *children's toys:* bicycles, tricycles, scooters, rocking horses, see saws, balls and kites
- *household 'supermarket':* secondary storage for surplus household groceries and supplies
- *holiday items:* suitcases, camping equipment and Christmas decorations
- *sports equipment:* tennis racquets, exercise equipment, bikes, skis, balls, golf and fishing
- *gardening equipment:* tools, mower, hoses and fertiliser.

Note it!

Make a list of your big fat categories and subcategories and create new ones as you discover things along the way.

Chunk it down

Work drawer by drawer, shelf by shelf until the entire garage contents are in their containers. Be ruthless with anything that has just been hanging around, unused and unloved. In such limited primary storage space everything must earn its right to stay. The entire garage should take you a few hours to fully reorganise. Remember that you can do just one subcategory any time you have a spare eight minutes. Just set the timer and go, go, go!

Step 4: elimin8

Eliminate as much as you can by asking the following critical questions of each item you are unsure about:

- Do I use you? If so, how often? When was the last time? When will be the next time?
- Do I need you?

- Do I really want you?
- Do I love you?

Most household items stored in garages are really items that should have left long ago. They are just more 'delayed decisions' awaiting their final send-off. Well, decision time has arrived! Make good use of your 'Bin it', 'Gift it', 'Sell it' and 'Move it' containers, then set limits on what will be stored in primary and secondary garage storage space. How many screwdrivers, fishing rods, bicycles, spare parts and soccer balls are enough?

Greg's grungy garage

Greg pulled into his driveway in his new car. All red and shiny, brand spanking new, just off the showroom floor! He lifted the door on his garage and carefully drove in. He opened his door to get out and already he knew he had a problem: he couldn't get out! Clutter and stuff had built up in the garage and there was only a narrow parking space left. The new golf clubs he got for his birthday stood next to his old set and to the other side was the even older set that he hadn't used for years. Greg shut the car door and reversed out again. His grungy garage had to go!

First job was a phone call to book a charity van to come and collect some things he knew he was ready to give away. They were coming the next day so he now had a deadline to meet. He liked that! He set to work placing items for the charity van on his front porch. He could see as he went along that there was a lot of rubbish that he needed to throw away, so he ordered a small skip and to his delight it was on its way. Within a short time he filled the skip and the porch looked like a charity shop! He found that creating deadlines and having places for his stuff to go motivated him to complete the job. By the end of the day, the shiny new red car had claimed its rightful position back in the garage!

 # Step 5: alloc8

Allocate containers and locations for what you are keeping. The advantage now is that you can see exactly how much stuff and space you have. The trick is to match the stuff with the space.

Organise your garage by allocating space by person, by function (such as car care, gardening or painting), or by type or shape of item (such as sprays, bottles, jars and cans). The choice is yours, and you can combine them. Do whatever makes sense to you.

Now would be a good time to get rid of all the storage leftovers from the house and invest in some suitable storage tailored to your needs.

Note it!

How are you going to allocate the space in your garage? Do you prefer to organise by person, by function, by type or shape of item, or by a combination of these? Consider everybody's needs, look at what you are working with and make a decision. Measure the space and decide on the containers that would best suit.

Storage smarts for garages

Refer to masterclass 4: getting a handle on hardware for a quick refresher, if necessary. When organising your garage consider the amount of storage space you have and your priorities. Create separate storage stations for big fat categories such as painting or car care.

CAUTION

Once you put things into a sealed box to place in the garage, it's most unlikely the box will ever be opened again. Go back to your elimination questions to really make sure that the items you are about to store are earning their right to stay.

Here are some guidelines for garage storage.

Peak hour
Organise your vehicles:

- Arrange vehicle parking to best suit the size of the car(s) and frequency of entry and exit.
- Place dust protectors over vehicles that are not used frequently.
- Use sensors to detect how close a vehicle gets to walls and cupboards.
- Use barriers to prevent vehicles hitting walls and cupboards.
- Consider installing electric doors for easy access.

Hot-rod heaven
Organise your car-care products:

- Set up a car-care station for everything you need for your cars.
- Keep car cleaning products on shelves or together in a bucket ready for action.
- Place car accessories on shelves.

Follow the drill
Organise your tools:

- Power tools should be stored in their original boxes, where possible, and placed on shelves or in cupboards.
- Pegboards are great for tools that are used on a regular basis.
- Tool boxes can hold a whole set of tools and are portable.

Pegboards are great for tools that are used on a regular basis

- Ladders can hang from hooks, rest on rafters or lean against walls.

One coat or two?

Organise your painting equipment:

- Paint should be stored in cans turned upside down to prevent skin forming.
- Don't store small quantities of paint. Decant to a smaller container or let it dry out and dispose of it.
- Keep a colour sample and the formula for paint colours you have used.
- Keep all painting equipment, such as brushes, rollers, trays, sandpaper and drop sheets, together.
- If you are doing some painting yourself, calculate the paint you need accurately, as leftover paint is rarely used but takes up storage space for years!

Don't play around

Organise your toys:

- The fact that the toys are out in the garage should tell you something!
- Store them in their original packaging where possible to protect and easily identify contents.
- Hang these on hooks on walls or store them on shelves.

Home shopping

Organise your household 'supermarket':

- Set up a household supermarket with small quantities of extra supplies of groceries.
- Use a shelving system or cupboard to store frequently used grocery items such as toilet paper, soap, washing detergent or canned tomatoes.
- Set a limit on what you buy.
- Rotate stock so items don't go stale.

Up, up and away!

Organise your holiday items:

- Use old suitcases or travel bags for garage storage to keep items dust free.

- Stack good suitcases inside each other and place them on shelves between trips.
- Create a camping station for all camping gear.

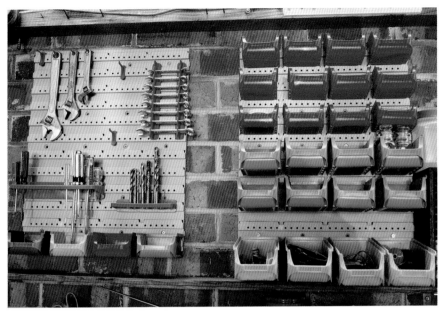

Store equipment on your garage walls

It's your serve!

Organise your sporting equipment:

- Hooks, racks and shelving cater to most sporting gear.
- Keep each sport separate with a station for each.
- Keep bike helmets within easy reach of children.

Dig a bit deeper

Organise your gardening equipment:

- Place long-handled items on racking or hooks.
- Short-handled items can go on pegboards with shape outlines to ensure return.
- Pesticides and chemicals should be placed out of reach of children on high shelving or in locked cupboards.

- Keep seeds in their packets and place them in containers on shelves.
- Gardening gloves can be placed in zip-lock bags to keep spiders out of them.

Roadworks ahead
Garage cautions:

- Keep poisons, pesticides and other dangerous items out of reach of children.
- Keep items off concrete floors as damp rises.
- Be mindful of water damage if the garage floods.
- Garages are not usually as well insulated or tightly sealed against weather conditions as houses so be careful of what you store. Temperature extremes, damp, heat and mildew can cause items to rust, warp, rot or corrode.

 Step 6: activ8

Finish it all off and put everything in its place:

- Give the garage a thorough clean, including light fittings and exhaust fans. Your garage should look like the ones you admire in magazines: fresh, clean and welcoming.
- Place items into their new locations, adjusting and adding storage if necessary. Label containers.
- Decide how much you want to have out on benches. Aim for the least amount possible. Items on garage benches take up valuable working space.
- Lastly, add a few decorator accessories to give the garage your personal touch.

Step 7: evalu8

Well done—you've finished the 'Do it' phase! You can now stand back and admire your results and measure them against your vision and the goals you set for yourself. It's time to get your camera out to take your 'after' photos. Compare them with your 'before' photos. *Wow!* What a difference! Go back to the notes you took in the 'Plan it' phase and note your answers to the following questions.

Note it!

- Have your frequent frustrations been addressed?
- Have you achieved your vision and your goals?
- Does your garage physically, functionally and emotionally please you?

If you say 'no' to any of these questions, make adjustments now or make a note to follow up within seven days. Continue to evaluate your garage and make changes as your lifestyle and circumstances change.

Review it Step 8: celebr8

No garage is going to keep itself looking the way yours does right now. You need to add regular garage cleaning and maintenance to your home care schedule. So let's quickly make a list of the tasks that need to be done to keep your garage humming. Here is an example of timely tasks for garages. Use this list or create your own.

Timely tasks for garages

Daily	Weekly	Monthly	Quarterly
Clear clutter	Empty bins	Declutter garage	Review shelving and storage
	Clean surfaces and floors	Clean cars	Clean refrigerators and freezers

Lock it in!

Once you have completed your own task list, add the tasks to your home care schedule. You will need to lock in a time to complete each task to maintain your new-look garage.

Raise the bar!

It's time to set new standards, new rules and new rituals to maintain your clean, organised and functional garage.

Keep your 'before' and 'after' photos handy to remind yourself of how far you have come and to see the new standard you have set. Create a few new rules such as: 'I never dump things in the garage', 'I always put things away after using them' and 'I do an in8minute tidy-up every Sunday before dinner'.

String a few tasks together to create a few new rituals. Your monthly garage ritual could be something like this:

- Move the cars out of the garage.
- Use the outdoor blower to clean the floor.
- Clean the cars and return them to the garage. Ahhh—the car is enjoying its new home!

Create new rituals to guide you through holidays and any other stressful time periods or tasks.

Maintain it!

Now all you need to do is follow your home care schedule and live up to your new standards. It will be easy to achieve with your fresh, clean garage as your foundation.

> **Note it!**
>
> I have completed my timely tasks for garages and locked times into my home care schedule.
> My new rules are: _____
> My new rituals are: _____

Congratulations! It's time to celebrate. You did it! You have created a garage that is clean, organised and functional. It's time to collect your reward for completing this room. Book in a massage, have coffee with friends, go to a show or just have a bath! You deserve it!

If you didn't leave the garage until last and you are ready for another room, turn to the relevant page and motor on!

Acknowledgements

From Stuffed to Sorted was written with the help of many people, and I would like to particularly thank the following.

My brother Harry literally gave up six weeks of his life to be my writing support buddy. He worked by my side tirelessly, selflessly and lovingly until the manuscript was fit for submission. Thank you, Harry. I am eternally grateful for your precious gift of time.

Team Wiley, my publishing team, have been wonderful and Lucy Raymond, Alice Berry and Elizabeth Whiley have been instrumental in providing feedback and keeping me to task and on time. Editor Sandra Balonyi was a delight to work with while she formatted and corrected the manuscript of its imperfections. I am so pleased with the book's final look and feel. Thank you.

My family has been a constant source of strength and encouragement. My husband David took over all the household duties and simply allowed me to be 'absent' during the writing process. Knowing everything was in good hands gave me the head space I needed. Thank you. My mother Helen has given me a lifetime of believing in me, loving me and supporting me in all I do. Thanks for providing all our sustenance while we were busy writing at your dining-room table. I wish Dad was still here to share in the joy. My children David, Michelle and Amanda, their partners and my grandchildren are a constant source of pride and joy. My brother Peter is on constant call while he continues to manage my web world. Thanks for all you do for me, often at a moment's notice!

My clients and workshop participants have generously shared their organising challenges and frustrations. You opened your hearts, souls, homes and offices to me and allowed me into your lives. Your contribution to my life and to this book is immeasurable. This book is for you and it is an honour and privilege to know you.

Brigitte Hinneberg co-authored *Paper Flow: your ultimate guide to making paperwork easy* and helped me bring the Paper Flow system to the world. Thank you for sharing my first authorship journey. *Paper Flow* has already helped thousands of people throughout the world sort their paperwork.

My friends and business associates have rallied behind me and given me the space required to concentrate on writing this book. I so appreciate your support and understanding.

I am very blessed to be surrounded by such wonderful people. Thank you one and all.

Image credits

p. ii, 2, 14, 16, 69 (bottom), 88, 91, 180, 197: © MaryAnne Bennie <www.in8.com.au>; p. 98: © Shaynna Blaze/Blank Canvas Interiors <www.shaynnablaze.com>; p. 60, 126, 170 © Albert Comper, supplied by Shaynna Blaze; p. 112, 120, 121, 122: products supplied by Décor Australia <www.decor.com.au>; p.160: © Gabrielle Di Stefano/Elements of Style <www.elementsofstyle.com.au>; p. 186, 195: © GarageSmart <www.garagesmart.com.au>; p. 36, 43 (top), 69 (top), 109, 112 (top), 115 (top), 119: © Häfele Australia Pty Ltd <www.hafele.com.au>; p. 86: © Howard's Storage World <www.hsw.com.au>; p. v, 17, 20, 30, 34, 45, 46, 48, 58, 110, 111, 112 (bottom), 114, 116, 120, 121, 122, 140, 142, 143, 148, 203: © Sash Ilievski/Desiren Photography <www.desiren.com.au>; p. 43 (bottom): © InaDRAWER Pty Ltd <www.inadrawer.com.au>; p. 78, 139: © Wardrobe World <www.wardrobeworld.com.au>; p. 39, 40, 42, 44, 115 (bottom): © Tom Wilson <www.howtorenovatewell.com>.

home
office
life
organising

About in8 home office and life organising

in8® Pty Ltd is a professional organising company founded by MaryAnne Bennie. The **in8steps** and **Paper Flow** systems were created by MaryAnne to help people sort their stuff and their paperwork simply, easily and sustainably. In addition to simple systems, some people require additional assistance, so in8 offers the following:

- resources and tools for organising your home, your office and your life
- newsletters and blogs with up-to-the-minute information and a touch of inspiration
- organiser training for individuals and professional organisers
- in-house assistance using **in8steps** and **Paper Flow** certified consultants and trainers.

in8 specialises in developing systems around people. Personal values and identity are important and are respected and nurtured at all times. in8 works together with you to build systems that get you up and running in the short term and that evolve and change with you through the long term.

For more information go to: <www.in8.com.au>; <www.paperflow.com.au>; and for additional support for *Paper Flow* — the book — go to <www.paperflowbook.com>.

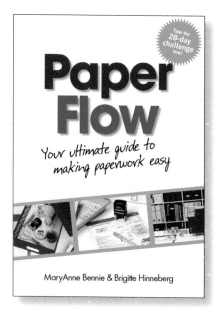

Paper Flow: your ultimate guide to making paperwork easy

Paper Flow is a beautifully simple, tried-and-tested system for handling your paperwork. This easy-to-follow guide is for everyone who handles the paper of life. Households, home businesses, small businesses and corporate employees will all benefit from having their paper flow.

In just ten minutes per day, the Paper Flow system will allow you to:

- deal with any piece of paper within seconds
- conquer routine tasks like paying bills, handling correspondence and filing
- manage projects at home or work, be it a renovation, tax return, holiday or work assignment.

Sit back and let the paper flow in, through and out of your life forever!

Available where books and ebooks are sold.

Paper Flow 28-day Challenge

The Paper Flow 28-day Challenge will help you establish a system for managing all of your paperwork. As featured in the best-selling book *Paper Flow*, this system is a beautifully simple, tried-and-tested way to deal with all the paper that enters our lives. The 28-day Challenge is your step-by-step guide to putting Paper Flow to work in any setting.

Everybody will benefit from taking the Paper Flow 28-day Challenge: households, students, executives, home-based or mobile businesses, mums and dads, frequent travellers, retirees, empty-nesters and more!

Available as an ebook from all good ebook retailers.